CONNECTION MARKETING

Convert the fairy tales of NETWORK MARKETING into SUCCESS that pays MORE THAN MONEY

FRAN BOORMAN

Published by Salbor Ltd

fran@fran.global
www.fran.global

Ordering Information:
Quantity sales. Special discounts are available on quantity purchases by corporations, associations, and others. For details, contact the author at the address above.

CONTENTS LIST

“*Fran Boorman embodies the true spirit of today's home-based entrepreneurs. She's part of a new breed of Leader who realises that it's not just about the size of your watch or how shiny your car is. Fran demonstrates that there is a deeper, more meaningful, and far more palatable reason for success. By sharing that success with others they too may have an avenue to achieve their goals. I am glad not to be a lone voice in the pursuit of a more believable way of working, and reason for doing so.*

The culture and people-first approach Fran takes in her business has won her many friends, as well as verifiable success. In this brave and thought-provoking book she helps us look beyond the noise that traditionally has dominated our space. Whilst she won't claim to have got to the peak of her journey, I've no doubt she'll use the contents of this book as a blueprint for further success.

Don't read this book in the hope of finding the quick and easy fixes or rewards with the least amount of effort. Do read this if you want some rational perspectives and wise insights. You will learn a mindset that can help build a sustainable and long-term culture. You can build once, build big, and build to last a lifetime.”

–WES LINDEN
Top-Ranking Leader; Amazon Best Selling Author; Host of The Mastermind Event

“*This intelligent, mature book leads the way for change. Fran's perspective is enlightening and will inspire the reader to take a better approach with their network marketing business. I particularly love the colourful analogies and real life experiences Fran shares as she guides the reader to a better business approach for the times we are in.*”

–DANIEL PRIESTLEY
4 Times Best Selling Author, Leader in Entrepreneurial Thinking

“This little book made me re-evaluate my own business. In her succinct and gentle tones, Fran digs deep to tell a personal tale of business success...and it resonates because of its engaging charm and outright honesty. Her story is as much about being a purposeful human as it is about marketing. And best of all it's rhetoric-free! It all seems so obvious now I've read it.”

–HOWARD SAUNDERS
Retail Futurist

“Having been involved in the world of network marketing for over a decade, it is clear that we are at a pivotal moment: the advent of peer to peer selling and the internet is challenging the traditional network marketing model. Now, more than ever, we need to go back to the core foundations that our industry was built upon: people - their social interactions, their personal connections and their motivations.

In this book Fran provides a rigorous analysis of what is going on in the world around us and how the time are changing for network marketers.

This isn't is another network marketing book preaching theory! It is stuffed full of anecdotes and learnings from what Fran has practised with considerable success in her business. It is written to provoke thought and to demonstrate the true value of what network marketing has to offer people all over the globe in the future.

This is a book about change - change at a personal level for the reader, and at an industry level for us all. Anyone who is serious about building a sustainable network marketing business for the future should read it.”

– ANDREW LINDSAY MBE
Network Marketing CEO

“*The world has changed and is changing still. Through Fran's unique experience and deep understanding, she takes you on a journey to discover the driving forces behind the new generation workforce - what they want and how you can connect.* Connection Marketing *is an engaging, educated,* ‘must read’ *for anyone in the Network Marketing industry. It's a thought provoking glimpse into the new world of business and power of connection for those who aren't connected......yet.*”

– CAROL SINFIELD
Top-Ranking Network Marketing Leader

“*I like books written by people who have actually done the work, people who actually walk the walk. I like books from people who've got a few bruises along the way where they've made mistakes and aren't afraid to hide that. I like this book because Fran has written it from real life experience.*

This is a no-holds barred and honest account of how to connect and how to make your network marketing business work. It doesn't tell you that everything is great all the time, and there are parts of it which were so true, they made me wonder why nobody had written about it before.

Buy the book and, most importantly, take action once you've read it. Be like Fran!”

– STEFAN THOMAS
Author of ‘Business Networking for Dummies’ and ‘Instant Networking’

“*Fran's book is great food for thought, and a must for thriving in the future of Network Marketing.*”

– DIANA PAGE
Top-Ranking Network Marketing Leader

"*Author, mother and professional network marketer Fran Boorman has created a powerful blueprint for anyone who has asked: "Can network marketing work for me?" "How can I be myself and build authentically?" "What are the skills I need to create a legacy?" She has given each of us a powerful roadmap, now it's up to us to take action.*"

– KYLE AND KIERSTON KIRSCHBAUM
Top-Ranking Network Marketing Professionals and US Leaders

THE CHALLENGE

[Chapter 1] THE FAIRY TALE OF NETWORK MARKETING

You probably joined network marketing for money. I'm going to show you how focusing on money is holding you back.

You probably also feel nervous, uncomfortable and almost 'dirty' when you offer your business to your friends and family. Many of us don't tell most people about it at all. For those people brave enough to talk openly about network marketing, they often find their excitement is misread and scares people off. I am going to show you how to build such a strong connection you will want to tell the world and the world will want to listen. In fact, I will be bold enough to say, the world will also want to follow you.

To do this we need to stop looking for quick fix magic pills and easy to teach skills. We need to start asking better questions about why we are not succeeding so we can find better answers. To do this we need to learn about a new way of marketing that has the power to change everything... Connection Marketing.

Our first fairy tale

There is a scene from *Peter Pan* when Wendy Darling and her brothers are sitting at the table for their first meal in Neverland. Peter shouts, "Dig in" and the Lost Boys dive into what appear to be empty bowls with such excitement and glee. The new kids around the table are confused and frustrated. They are starving hungry, but they can't see the delicious food to pick up.

Sound familiar? This is how many people in network marketing feel. They are sitting around the table desperate to get stuck in but they don't know how. The Darlings ask, in fact, they beg the lost boys to let them into the secret of how they are satisfying themselves. Eventually, they tell Wendy to simply believe, to effectively change her mindset so she can see the wonderful fruits they can see. Well, this is a fairy tale, so almost magically the Darlings grow the belief and they too can join the phenomenal feast.

No doubt you have been told many times that to be successful in network marketing we simply need to have belief in ourselves, our company, and our products. We need to have good posture and share that confidently with the people around us. But what does it actually mean and how do we achieve this? We are sold the 'dream of network marketing' like it is some sort of fairy tale. But it is not, and simply being told to believe is not enough.

No doubt you have also been told that to achieve success in network marketing you need to communicate with people what you do and what your company has to offer. But once again this does not cut it anymore. We are now constantly communicated at from every direction, including through social media, news feeds, email bombardments, and messaging apps. There is so much noise that none of us has a clue what to listen to anymore; all we know is that we can't listen to it all! Simply telling people about our network marketing business is not enough either.

We need to stop blabbering out our fairy tales and start getting real with people. But what do we tell them? In fact, what do we tell ourselves? How do we explain to people this amazing gift that we have? How do we teach people to sit at the table and eat with us?

Connection Marketing is about addressing a new world and maturing the network marketing industry.

> What we have to offer is so powerful and so perfect for the world we live in, but we need to learn how to serve it to that world.

We need to turn our fairy tale into a reality for you, for me and for all the other people who we can impact. Connection Marketing is about measuring our success not simply through the fairy tale of retiring on beaches. It is about appreciating that what we do is greater than one person's earnings; network marketing has the power to change people's lives in so many ways.

We live in a world more connected than ever before, yet people feel lonely. It is a world full of opportunity, yet people feel unfulfilled and unable to access it. With network marketing we have a vehicle to step above these challenges and create a community, which unites people. We have an opportunity to be part of something greater than ourselves; something meaningful and worthwhile.

> Our real value is not money, it is CONNECTION.

When we start trading in connection we harness our real power. Business will be so much more fun to build that we won't want to be sitting on a beach twiddling our thumbs anymore, because together we will be changing the world!

So, pull up a chair to the table of network marketing and let's start the feast together.

Welcome to Connection Marketing.

My fairy tale of discovery

Let me share with you why I want to tell you this story. I have been involved in network marketing for a decade. I have grown a business, which is consistently recognised as one of the fastest growing in our company. But unlike many other high achievers, I am not a machine. I am not so driven that I can telephone hundreds of people a month and pitch to everyone in sight. In this way, I am a pretty average person.

I started as a pregnant Mum-to-be and I thought the reason I was doing my business was so I didn't have to go back to work for someone else after maternity leave. I achieved my business financial goal before my first baby was born, but then everything changed. I went from being able to build a business on my agenda to being stripped of all my freedom. I became a willing servant to this beautiful bundle of joy. If my business was going to survive and if I was going to survive, I had to change significantly.

Why my business survived and flourished

I made a good start to my business before my son was born, but it was nothing exceptional. Until that point, I was dutifully following the traditional fairy tale network marketing system. I was being professional, showing my presentation to as many people as possible and working the numbers game. That was never going to work around a little person who needed feeding every three to four hours. I had to change something to keep my business growing.

I started developing my Connection Marketing approach, which continues to grow today. Rather than slowing down, my business started to accelerate and my customer base grew. More than anything else, my team grew with connected team members who were as engaged and excited as me.

Why my business helped me survive

What I didn't expect was my network marketing business to rescue me from almost certain insanity. I was besotted with my baby, but I found becoming a mother stripped me of all my identity. I went from being an independent woman to someone who couldn't even choose when she went to the toilet!

This is when my network marketing business saved me in more ways than money ever could. It gave me something engaging and exciting that was my own; something to build around and to give me a lot of time with my children. It gave me my independence, a feeling of value and self-worth. This was so much more valuable to me than anything money can buy. It was from this experience that I started trading in what has now become known as Connection Marketing.

Twist to my story

As with all good stories there is a twist. As a child I was exposed to some rather exceptional circumstances which shaped me, giving me an insight that undoubtedly helped me disproportionately to other people. My father, keenly supported by my incredible mother, is an exceptionally successful businessman. Through my childhood Mum and Dad grew a significantly large business from scratch. Today it is of a magnitude that enables them to provide sound employment for thousands of people. My Dad was honoured by the Queen of England with an Order of the British Empire for his contribution to business and industry.

The fairy tale this might paint in your mind is that Daddy helped his precious little daughter build her business, waving his magic wand to fix all her problems. In fact, it is quite the opposite. What I learned from my father was that fairy tales don't exist. I learned the stark reality of hard work and what it really takes to achieve. To ensure my success, Dad was more likely to place obstacles in my way, rather than help me over them. That is how I learned to overcome challenge.

The secret magic I gained from this unusual upbringing was an incredible insight into what it takes to truly be successful in business. It is only in recent years that I have begun to appreciate how much I learned from growing up in an environment that was subtly electric.

By having unlimited access to my father and his peers I was able to study what made these people different. I wanted to find out why they succeeded when so many other people didn't. Surprisingly, what I was taught about success in network marketing did not translate into my father's world. I started questioning and investigating why what we teach is so different from the reality of these hugely successful people. It was through this process that I started to understand and decode not simply the success of other people, but the success I was having. I am going to share with you much of what I have learned.

What is the Connection Marketing?

One of the favourite lessons I learned from my father is that...

> "every problem creates an opportunity"

This has become a mantra for my life and has served me very well. When I was faced with the huge challenge of becoming a mother I searched for the opportunities. I have learned to embrace change and use it as an accelerator for growth.

The world has never seen so much rapid change as in recent years. Technology, politics, business; there is constant huge change. For most people change makes them feel insecure and concerned. For me, I see opportunity.

In the first chapters of this book we are going to look at the changes impacting the network marketing industry and society. We will examine how they are going to create a perfect storm for our industry to harness massive opportunity. To move from an industry that tells fairy tales, to one that creates money and even greater value.

As an industry we can create something everyone craves, connection. The remainder of the book will examine how connection is the way forward for network marketing. It is achieved by engaging the 4Cs of connection; cause, culture, commit and communicate. By mastering the 4Cs you will be able to breakthrough to your network marketing success.

Warning: don't waste your time

I have seen thousands of network marketers devour hundreds of different personal development books. It is wonderful to see people's willingness to learn. I have not been so virtuous. As an awkward dyslexic, reading a book is more of a performance for me. Ironically, I believe this has contributed to my success. It takes such a lot of effort that I am always determined to make it worthwhile. When I get a book, I don't simply read it; I study it. I want to get all the value out that my time deserves. Most importantly, I put it into action.

I hope you enjoy this book and if you are reading for entertainment that is great. But if you are reading to make a difference then I have some bad news for you... you may be wasting your time. The value of this book only comes when you put into action what you learn. If you commit to learning and implementation then a break through awaits you.

Some more bad news... they are no quick fixes or magic pills. Some of the work that lies ahead will be challenging. It will force you to step out of your comfort zone, perhaps in ways you haven't before. However, you will be making big strides forward that can go on to impact you in a significant way. Please embrace the process. Find the joy in the effort and sense of achievement. Know you are starting something so exciting it can change your world and a lot more.

[We need people to deeply connect with our businesses so there is the desire to do what it takes.]

[Chapter 2]
THE NETWORK MARKETING INDUSTRY

Our next fairy tale is from Roald Dahl's book, *Witches.* An eclectic mix of people descend on a hotel conference room, where rows of chairs are lined up. Everyone files in and takes their place. They are excited to hear from the Grand High Witch about how they are going to take over the world. Yes, it is a network marketing recruitment evening, but maybe like the witches in Dahl's conference room, everything isn't quite as it seems.

Filled with distributors and their guests, everyone is ready to hear what all the fuss is about. When it comes to the testimonial section the first distributor stands up. He is introduced as having reached the first level of promotion in the company and is asked to share his story.

"My name is Bruce, I was an accountant and what I like best about the business is that I have been able to leave my accounting job and have all the free time I want".

The second person stands up and says, "My name is Susan, I work in healthcare and what I like about this business is that I get paid even when I don't work"... and so it continues.

I know all network marketing plans are different, but I am pretty sure the income from the early first stage of promotion is not enough to securely give up a professional day job. I know Bruce, he is a clever guy. He is an accountant as well, so why does he claim such an absurd thing? Why do the rest of us smile, nod and applaud him!? As for Susan, she is a hard worker, and doing this business has made her feel valued and fulfilled in a way her day job didn't. So, why does she claim what she liked best was the time when she wasn't actually building her business? When did these perfectly rational, intelligent people become such good fairy tale storytellers? What did we do to these people to make them peel off their masks to expose their 'witch'?

The evening usually ends with the Grand High Witch host, a leader in our business, sharing their story. In their journey to become the Grand High Witch there is no doubt they have become a pretty remarkable person. It is natural that we all feel inspired by them.

They sell us the fairy tale of network marketing and residual income. The business has given them money and freedom; they no longer have to work for someone else. So, here is my question, why have they travelled the length of the country to prance around a hotel room late in the evening? If their business has done for them what we tell people it can, they should be draped on a sun lounger on the other side of the world, watching their bank account tick up and up with every passing second.

> The real irony of network marketing is the story we tell and the lives we lead alongside the stories.

When it comes to communicating the benefits of our business model, it is like we are tearing off the mask of our normality to expose a witchy cult of misled people!

Hopefully this vision has made you chuckle and please forgive me for a little creative license. The people I talk about are pretty phenomenal. They are the knights in shining armour of our story who are rising up against the evil of a repressive, mediocre world. But for them and for us to slay the dragons and rescue all the princesses, we are going to need to change the way we communicate and ultimately, the way we connect with people. We are going to need to stop trading in stories of financial currency and start trading in something more powerful.

The story of network marketing

To begin the story of our industry, let's first set the scene of where we are in the evolution of network marketing and understand how we got here. Like the growth of a child through to adulthood, our industry is going through some amazing and exciting changes, driven by some impressive people.

■ The Toddlers

We started with the early pioneers of the industry. They were the resilient, determined toddlers learning to walk. If they fell down, they got back up again. They didn't necessarily know what they were doing, but they were of the disposition that they simply kept trying until they found their way.

■ The Teenagers

Once the industry had found its feet, it was time to start understanding itself and its place. Those were the days when we were testing our boundaries and the people around us. We thought we had all the answers and would club together in a strop if anyone didn't agree with us. Those were the days when we used to cover objections with clever comebacks. If someone asked, "Is it a pyramid scheme?" we would respond with, "Actually, your job is more like a pyramid scheme - in fact your job is a scam - not my business". Like any teenager, we needed to defend ourselves while we worked out who we were and where our place was in the world.

■ The Students

Having survived the teenage years, the next logical step in our growth was to go to our metaphorical university, to grow up and get an education. This is when the industry skilled up and started to become a profession. We started to learn our trade and to work logically. Network marketing organisations across the world have made huge strides forward in creating comprehensive training programmes and resources.

All the skills someone needs to build a business are accessible and in theory anyone should now be able to succeed, but they don't.

This is where we have got to in the evolution of our industry and unsurprisingly, we are frustrated. We have evolved an amazing industry that is supported by systems and tools that should see an explosion of achievement, but it is not happening.

Now we need to mature as an industry and we are entering our adulthood. We would have not got here without the pioneers of the toddler days, the camaraderie of the teenage days and the teachers of the student days. Now the industry is ready for its next evolution.

■ The Young Adults

Today we emerge like confident young adults with skills and ambitions ready to take on the world. As we embark on our careers as educated professionals our job now is to start to work out who we really are and share that with the world. We must start to understand our values and beliefs. For the first time we can stand up in front of the masses and lead the way forward.

At this new dawning we need to appreciate that what we did in the past was incredibly valuable to get us to where we are today. We need to thank our pioneers who got us this far. However, to move forward we need to change and evolve again.

That means that we need to change the way we think and behave.

Asking the right questions

Whenever I am asked for advice by other network marketers, it is always about skills. "Please can you teach me a better recruiting script?", "What do you say in this situation?", "How do I teach my team to be more motivated?"

People want answers to succeed, but they want the answers in the form of a duplicatable skill. This is understandable because learning the skills of the student days has catapulted our industry forward significantly. However, those skills are not providing a good enough sustainable solution on their own any more. It is not because the answers are wrong; it is because the answers are not motivating action.

What we need to do is learn how to ask better questions. We need to be asking questions about how we motivate ourselves and our team to implement these skills.

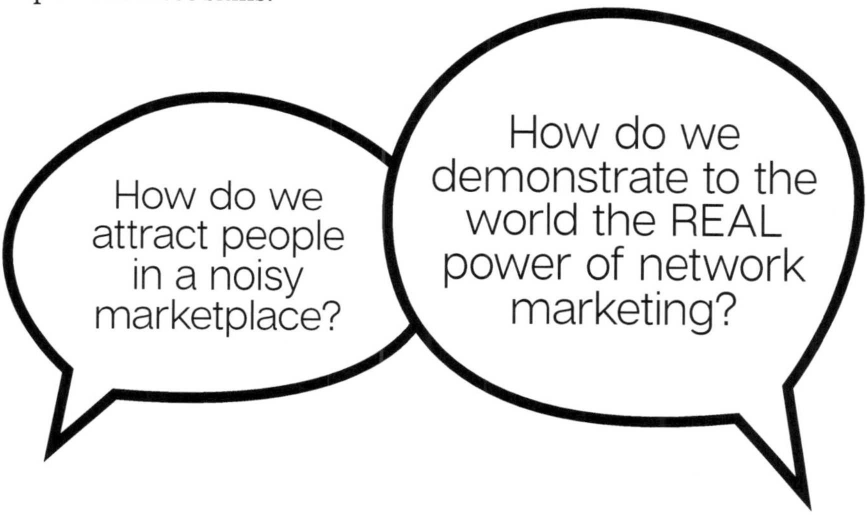

If we want our businesses moving forward, we need to ask questions which will have answers that send us in a new and better direction of adulthood.

The beginning of our young adulthood

As we begin this new era, let's first address the ironies we started with. Why do we tell these fairy tales and what stories should we be telling? Firstly, let's examine our Grand High Witches, our leaders. These are the people who bravely endured the toddler, teenage and student days. They talk about money because when they were pioneering this industry most people didn't understand what it was about. They needed to trade in a currency people did understand. They traded in the most universal currency; money.

Through sheer hard graft and dogged determination, they were able to generate great income streams. But these income streams were very different from those that people outside the industry understood. They were not linear incomes; in other words, do an hour of work and get paid for an hour. The income they generated was royalty or residual income based, which meant do an hour and get paid repeatedly for that work. This was a hard concept for people to grasp. To help explain it, our pioneers used the example of sitting on a beach and getting paid for doing nothing. They were so good and focused on telling this beach story that many of them began to believe it themselves.

However, if you have met any of these early industry leaders you will know that while they might enjoy being on a beach that is not enough for them. They are so excited and connected to their businesses that they are highly likely to be broadcasting a live stream to their teams while they feel the sand trickle between their toes. Network marketing needed this message to get to where it is today. However, now we need to step back and look at the real value of our businesses. What we have is so powerful and so remarkable that it makes beach lifestyle feel, quite frankly... dull!

Money attracts, but does not hold us

Over the years I have spoken to hundreds of network marketing distributors. I have always asked why they do the business, but I very rarely accepted their first answer. The first answer is normally the money reason of why they started the business; a little extra money to go on holiday, to pay off the loan, or for after school clubs. These answers explain why people joined in the first place, but they never really explain why they have continued - or in some cases not continued - to do the business.

You see there are three types of people in our business and each one

proves that money is not the main motivating factor.

Firstly, you have the achievers. This is the smallest group. They have earned the money they wanted and achieved their goals. Often, they have earned more than they originally hoped for. If money was the main motivator they would have scarpered and gone to enjoy their financial and time freedom 'on the beach', but they don't. They are still actively involved in the business and continue to go above and beyond.

The second group are those people not earning what they want from the business, yet they still appear completely committed. They turn up to events, they talk passionately about the company, and they often go as far as wearing company merchandise at all times. They have a huge passion for the industry, even if they are not yet achieving what they say they want to from it. I used to think it was the dream of what they could achieve, that made so many people commit to network marketing. But if you dig deep and get people to honestly open up, this is not why they come back.

And what about those people who don't hang around or the ones who simply dip their toe in every so often? This last group is probably the largest in the industry. They are the people who physically or psychologically quit before they get near to what they joined for. Our businesses are proven systems and they are proven to work. If someone really wanted and really needed to achieve a financial goal, they could. It might not be easy, but if the desire is strong enough they can do what it takes. When someone quits you can remind them of the money goal they joined for, what they wanted, but very rarely does this actually win them back. They shrug their shoulders and return to their day jobs.

If it is money that was the main and only motivator we wouldn't see these three scenarios. If you are reading this book, it is highly likely you are in the first and second group. Do you know what really motivates you? What are the fairy tales you have been telling yourself?

We must attract not repel

One of the reasons why many people decide working overtime is a better strategy than network marketing is because of the way our industry is viewed by the public. We like to think the world is more educated about network marketing these days. In the teenage days, "Is it a pyramid scheme?" and other suggestively critical questions were part of everyday life for network marketers. So much so, that teaching responses to these criticisms was standard training. Accusations such as these have massively reduced, but we still have a lot more work to do.

Once, I attended an invitation only meeting of top young influencers from all different industries. Attendees were only invited on merit and we all knew the tough criteria we had been assessed on. We were all equals. As we welcomed and networked with each other, I received a reaction I had become accustomed to enduring.

I had gone into the room full of confidence and passionate about my industry. The first lady I met was a pleasure to talk with and she told me all about her business. In turn, when she asked about my business I explained that I was a network marketer. If the look of disgust on her face was not enough to tell me all I needed to know, then her actions finished it off. Completely subconsciously and without realising it, she took a massive step backwards away from me. You don't have to be an expert in reading body language to understand how she felt about our industry. From someone who a minute ago had been warm and engaging, she now couldn't move away from me quickly enough. And it was not only her; I was pleased to discover most people in the room had heard of network marketing, however in one way or another they all displayed a similar reaction.

It was not that I had been invited into a room of particularly negative people. I get this reaction in all different environments with all different types of people. No matter how much I try and sugar coat what I say, in many cases as soon as I mention network marketing there is some sort of 'pull back' reaction. I have such strong belief in our industry I can often win people back and change their view, but this is an issue we need to address as an industry. We need to change the way our industry is viewed by other people and to do that we need to work together.

I ended up working quite closely with this 'influencers group' and other people who had reacted negatively when I first met them. I have managed to change their views and many of them have gone on to become friends. After several open and honest discussions I asked why their initial reaction was so bad.

Interestingly, most of them didn't realise how visual their reaction was, but all of them admitted that their impression of our industry was very bad. When I asked why, I heard the same answer time and time again. It was based on their previous experiences of other network marketers where they felt they had been victims of pushy sales techniques. They told stories of being invited to meetings under false pretences and relentless sales attempts that felt desperate. The general feeling was that network marketers were 'money grabbing' and to be avoided at all costs!

We must accept our reality and learn to move forward from it. We must appreciate the thankless tasks and barrage of rejection that our mighty pioneers had to go through, but now is the time to move on. Now it is time to mature. "Be the change you want to see in the world". We need to change. This is not simply about skilling up. It is about changing who we are as an industry and maturing what we stand for.

We need to start attracting rather than repelling.

Can anyone do network marketing?

The network marketing industry now has the skills, training and systems in place so that in theory, anyone should be able to achieve success. We often hear that one of the beauties of network marketing is that anyone can do it. But is this really true? Can anyone and everyone be a network marketer? We often get frustrated by that third group of people who join our networks, but never actually get going. So, is this another fairy tale?

It is true that our businesses are very accessible to the average person. Pretty much anyone who can get their hands on a low joining fee is allowed to join and many do. But simply joining is not enough. It is also true that the skills someone needs to build a network marketing business can be learned by anyone. With enough time and support anyone can learn how to do what we do. But again that doesn't mean everyone will actually do it, or more over that most people achieve.

Years ago we approached the third group of people with the attitude of 'Some will, some won't, so what, who's next?' Ouch! Not the most empowering philosophy. While this was an important attitude in the pioneering days, we are now much more mature as an industry. For the last few years we have had a better strategy. We believe that our challenge is to teach network marketers better skills. The theory is that better skills will mean they are more confident and they will have more success. They will then earn money, realise how amazing our businesses are and commit completely for ever more. But this is not working either.

We need to find a better strategy. What we need to do is learn how to help people find a real desire to build a business with us. What really matters is someone's commitment to building a business. When they join they must want to take a step out from the crowd. When they start learning the skills they must want to change themselves. When they start visiting prospects they have to be willing to step out of their comfort zones. To be successful in network marketing, you must have enough motivation and desire to actually do it.

We need people to deeply connect with our businesses so there is the desire to do what it takes.

What it takes

The fairy tale we sell is of hypothetical pop stars. Network marketing is like spending a few hours writing a song that goes on to be a platinum record. You can sit back and enjoy the royalties for the rest of your life. While this is a nice analogy, I have never heard anyone go on to explain the full picture.

Never have they mentioned that along the way to writing their hit song they wrote countless other songs, which are binned. Or how they stood on the street in the cold busking. Or about how they got rejected from hundreds of record companies while surviving on baked beans huddled around an electric heater they can only afford to turn on for an hour a day!

The realities of network marketing might not be quite as harsh as that, but anyone who has tried it will know that it is no 'walk in the park'. It is hard work! Let's be realistic with each other. To be successful at network marketing you are going to need to speak to a lot of people. You are going to need to learn lots of new skills and be willing to make changes to yourself. You are going to need to go to events during the evenings and weekends. You are going to need to step out of your comfort zone. Heck, you might even have to give up scrolling though Facebook every evening! Generally, only once people have joined do they discover these truths!

But before you hand in your resignation we need to put these facts into context. Let me reassure you that what I am going to show you through *Connection Marketing* is how phenomenal this business is. So phenomenal that it makes trading all those hours, worth more than money can ever buy. There will be money in your network marketing journey and if you start trading in the Connection as an alternative currency there is a good chance there will be lots of money. But money will become a measure of your success, not the principle reason for doing it.

Money as a measure not motivator

As I sat with my father in his office, I was excited having returned from one of my first network marketing trainings. I am very close to my father and was excited to explore a new level in our relationship, approaching him as a fellow business owner. Written in my lovely new journal I had dutifully listed my goals and how much I wanted to earn from my business.

When I had been asked to write this down in my training I remember feeling awkward and unsure. The enthusiasm of the Grand High Witch that day had given me a borrowed confidence to write the list anyway. I had been taught to start talking to people about money. I had been encouraged to ask people what goals they had and how much money they needed to achieve them.

So, I asked my Dad, "Tell me, what are your goals? What is it you want to grow your business for?"

The reaction I got to this question was not what I expected. My Dad swivelled round in his chair, with a look of almost disgust on his face. He peered over his glasses and stated, "What a bloody stupid question.

Why are you asking me stupid questions?"

Lesson one of successful people; they say it how it is and talk in realities!

While it might have not been the most sensitive of responses, he had a point. I had never noticed my father sit down and create vision boards of the houses he wanted to buy or the cars he wanted to drive. Don't misunderstand me. He has a great lifestyle and all the typical rewards you expect. But these things were a result not a cause of his success. I quizzed some of his peers and for all of them money was a measure of success, but not the motivator.

At first, I concluded it was because of the scale of their businesses. Perhaps for the average person building a network marketing business, the motivations were different? But I also looked around at the leaders of our business. While they dutifully promoted the fairy tales of money goals, this was not reflected in the way they lived their lives, nor conducted their businesses.

As my business grew, I started to reflect on my motivations. I too, shared the 'time freedom and money' story but it was not true for me either. I didn't jump out of bed every morning excited to earn more money towards a Ferrari. I jumped out of bed excited about growing my business. Some nights I was so excited I hadn't even managed to get to sleep before it was time to jump out of bed!

What was motivating all these successful people?

More importantly, if we understood it, can we use this as a motivator for real success?

[Chapter 3] CURRENT SOCIETY

As Rapunzel sat in her tower gazing out of the large stone window, she could see for miles. In the distance beyond the forest, were communities of people all going about their business. At night she saw the glow of lights and activity. Occasionally, she admired firework displays of distant celebrations. She yearned to be part of them, but she couldn't. Rapunzel had everything going for her. She was intelligent, empathetic, beautiful and determined, but she was trapped and didn't know how to get out.

This is a tale as old as time and yet this is the life so many people live in today's society. The difference is, their window to the world isn't a stone opening, it's a screen. The world has never been more connected than it is today, yet people feel lonelier than ever. If there was a huge twist in a story, the twist of technology in our society must be the greatest.

We were granted the gift of devices that were meant to connect us and instead they isolated us. They have done such a good job of isolation that some people feel alone in their own tower, even when surrounded by other people. They are together, but alone. It is definitely not the 'happy ever after' ending, but that is because perhaps it is not the ending?

Let us consider for a moment why Rapunzel wanted to escape. In the tower she had a beautiful home with a fabulous view. She was well nourished and according to the fairy tale, she had ample books to read and hobbies to occupy her. She didn't have to slave away at manual labour to earn her keep; she was a lady of leisure. Maybe she was simply a high maintenance spoiled little princess!

What was she really missing...? Connection. Obviously, to make it a fairy tale, she wanted the connection of a dashing young prince, but I am pretty sure if anyone else had turned up she would have still accepted a ride out of there. Fundamentally, what she yearned for was that feeling of being with other people and not only her saviour prince. If he had whisked her off to his castle and stuck her in there with him, I think we all know the sequel to that story wouldn't have had a fairy tale ending.

No, Rapunzel went on to work with the people of her kingdom. She helped create a better society both for herself and the other people around her. What gave Rapunzel her 'happy ever after' was when she was part of something greater than herself and she felt connected with that.

So, look up from the pages of this book. Who can you see around you who is stuck in their tower? Or maybe it is you who is stuck? Maybe you are dangling half way out the window swinging from your hair, not quite able to feel the grass beneath your feet? But, do you hear the hoofs of that horse thundering through the forest towards you? That is the sound of your prince. That is the sound of network marketing.

> We live in a connected but lonely world.

The need for belonging

The 'Hierarchy of Needs' proposed in Abraham Maslow's 1943 paper, *A Theory of Human Motivation*[1] is one of the most popular frameworks in sociology. The paper looks at the essential needs of a human being to survive. The first basic needs for any human being are our physiological needs, essentially the need for food, water and air. Then come our safety needs and keeping out of harm's way. The third and most important need for a human being, is social belonging.

The way we have been approaching network marketing up until this stage is by trying to appeal to people's physiological and safety needs. We offer a financial solution that gives people the ability to provide food and shelter for them and their families. This was and continues to be a very virtuous thing to do. It is relevant and there will always be a place for us to talk about fulfilling these essential needs for people.

5 Self-actualization
[achieving individual potential]

4 Esteem
[from self and others]

3 Belonging
[being part of a group, love, affection]

2 Safety
[shelter, clothes, removal from danger]

1 Physiological
[health, food, sleep]

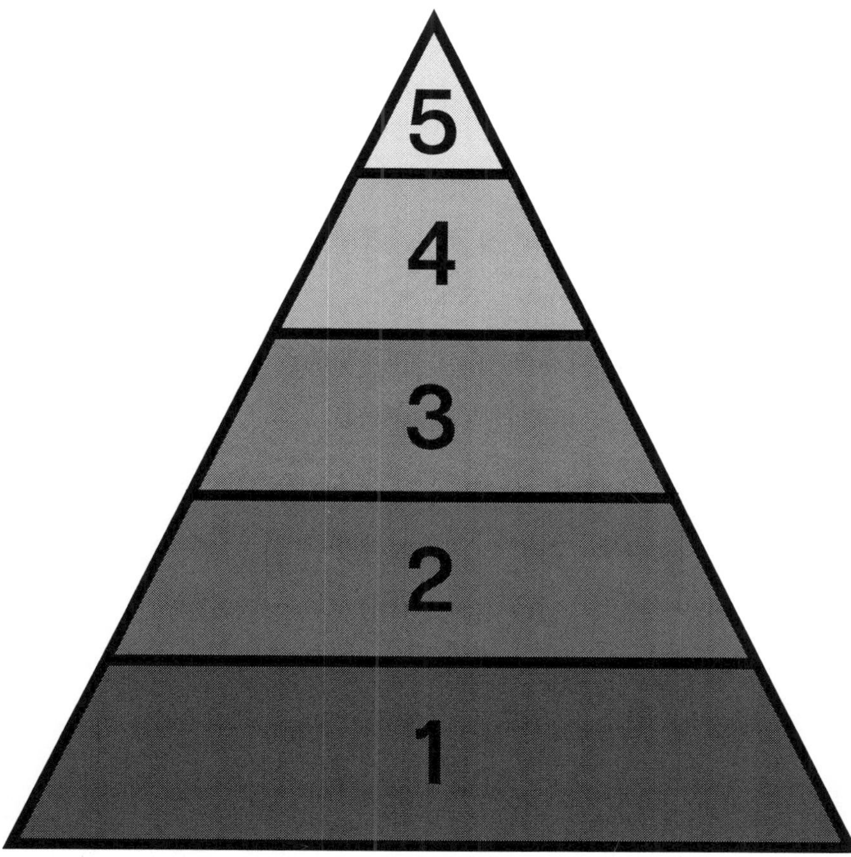

'The Hierarchy of Needs', Abraham Maslow, 1943

However, I feel this is now not enough. The way our world is now connected through technology has had many unexpected side effects, which appear to be creating a void. When we learn to harness this as an opportunity, I believe we will make a huge impact.

Dopamine addicted society

These days most people are scientifically addicted to their news feeds, text messages, Instagram posts and all sorts of other social media connections. Neuroscience studies have proven that when someone puts a post on Facebook they are literally crying out for connection. After making the post they may continue to scroll on for a bit or get on with something else, but what they always do is to come back to see how many 'likes' they have achieved. Why...? because when we see our post has been 'liked' it triggers our bodies to release the hormone dopamine.

This hormone is part of our brain's reward system and it makes us feel good. New York University professor Adam Alter, explained that, "When someone 'likes' an Instagram post, or any content that you share, it's a little bit like taking a drug. As far as your brain is concerned, it's a very similar experience".[2]

Now you can argue that by using social media we are connecting with more people more quickly, so surely this type of connection is a good thing? I disagree. When you 'like' someone's post you might feel you are connecting with them but you are not. When they log back in to check their post they are only interested in one thing... the number of 'likes', not who the 'likers' were.

The more 'likes' you get, the better you feel you have done and the more dopamine your brain will release. By 'liking' someone else's post you are making them feel good, but there is no real connection there.

Trapped looking at the whole world

Like Rapunzel stuck in her tower, with technology and social media we are showing people the world, but generally not showing them how they can access it. We have the most powerful tools at our fingertips, but most people don't know how to really use them. They have got stuck in their isolated tower and can't see the way out.

What makes it more frustrating is that it is not only to the horizon they can see, they can see the whole world. They know there is life out there, but they don't know how to access it. So, they surrender to a spiral of falling back on small dopamine kicks.

One fascinating thing about Rapunzel's story is that she never looked for a way out of her tower. For all the years she was trapped, she didn't think of lifting a few floorboards to see if there were stairs descending. She simply sat there waiting to be rescued. She was happy to haul up a fully-grown man and his armour on her locks, but she never thought about lowering her own petite self down!

I agree, of course, that if she had done this a few years earlier it wouldn't have made such a fairy tale ending, but isn't this the same with most people in our society? They could put down their mobile telephones and engage with people, but instead they are waiting for something. They are waiting for someone to grab their attention and show them how to connect.

If you look at all the disruptive technologies that have come to the market in recent times they are always about utilising technology to connect people. For example, Airbnb uses technology to connect people with a spare room to travellers. Uber connects people with a vehicle to those who need to get somewhere. All these companies do is use the technology to connect people. The companies who succeed in this new world are the ones who not only show people the world, but also show them how to access it. They show them how to make real human connections.

Generation Y

Gen Y are regarded as the babies born between 1977 to 1994[3] and according to the Direct Selling Association this group of people made up 50 percent of our industry in 2016[4]. They are also a key target market of future network marketers because as they continue with their careers and settle down with families, they are likely to need an extra income. But Gen Y are often considered a troubled generation.

Tim Urban in his November 2017, *Huffington Post* article described the challenges for this generation and why they are, "kinda unhappy" and "unfulfilled". He explained that Happiness = Reality – Expectation. The baby boomer parents of Gen Y had low expectations, living in a post-war world. The massive economic development of the 70s, 80s and 90s exceeded the expectations of these baby boomers. This made them almost sensationally happy. Therefore, they raised their Gen Y children with a "sense of optimism and unbounded possibility".[5] These children became adults believing they were special and would have a fulfilling career.

Happiness equals

REALITY **(minus)** EXPECTATION

Sadly, the reality proved to be below their expectation. Already their happiness equations weren't looking great. To make matters worse, they searched on social media for happiness and they only saw an edited version of everyone else's perfect lives.

Adam Alter joined the debate explaining, "Everyone presents the very best versions of their lives... What that means is, every time you look at someone's feed, you're getting only the very best aspects of their lives, which makes you feel like your life, in comparison with all its messiness, probably isn't as good. Seeing the best version of everyone else's life makes you feel deprived".[2] Arguably, the largest group of current and perspective network marketers feel unfulfilled, specifically in their careers.

The need for fulfilment is not a new phenomenon. Maslow in his, *Hierarchy of Needs* cited 'esteem' as the next human need after belonging.

Dale Carnegie appreciated that "we all crave appreciation and recognition and will do almost anything to get it".[6] Fulfilment is something that has always been important to people. Within the network marketing industry, we have often placed importance on recognition for achievement, but is this enough to make this generation feel fulfilled?

The Deloitte 2017, *Millennial Survey* showed a strong theme about how this generation are keen to gain fulfilment from feeling they are part of something that is worthwhile. Much of this was related to the businesses they engage with. "Almost nine in ten, 86 percent, believe the success of a business should be measured in terms of more than only its financial performance… by involving employees in such initiatives, employers seem to be boosting Millennials' sense of empowerment… This is an important point for businesses to acknowledge because it offers a platform from which to build each employee's sense of purpose and, ultimately, a more engaged workforce".[7]

Generation Z

Gen Z are regarded as the babies born between 1995 and later. It was no coincidence that Afghan teen Malala Yogsafzai became the youngest person to win the Nobel Peace Prize at aged 18. She is an early Gen Z and this generation want to change the world.

The next cohort of young people who will be coming into the workplace are looking for more than simply a job. These exciting young people will be our future distributors and we need to start attracting them now.

"Gen Z is excited about how they can make the world a better place, as well as how they can partner with their employers in doing so", David Stillman and his Gen Z son, Jonah Stillman explained in their popular book, *Gen Z @ Work*.[8]

But it is not only about employers.

Arne Duncan, former United States Secretary of Education asked Gen Z, "What are you planning to do to change the world?" In the top three responses were, "Start my own business".[8]

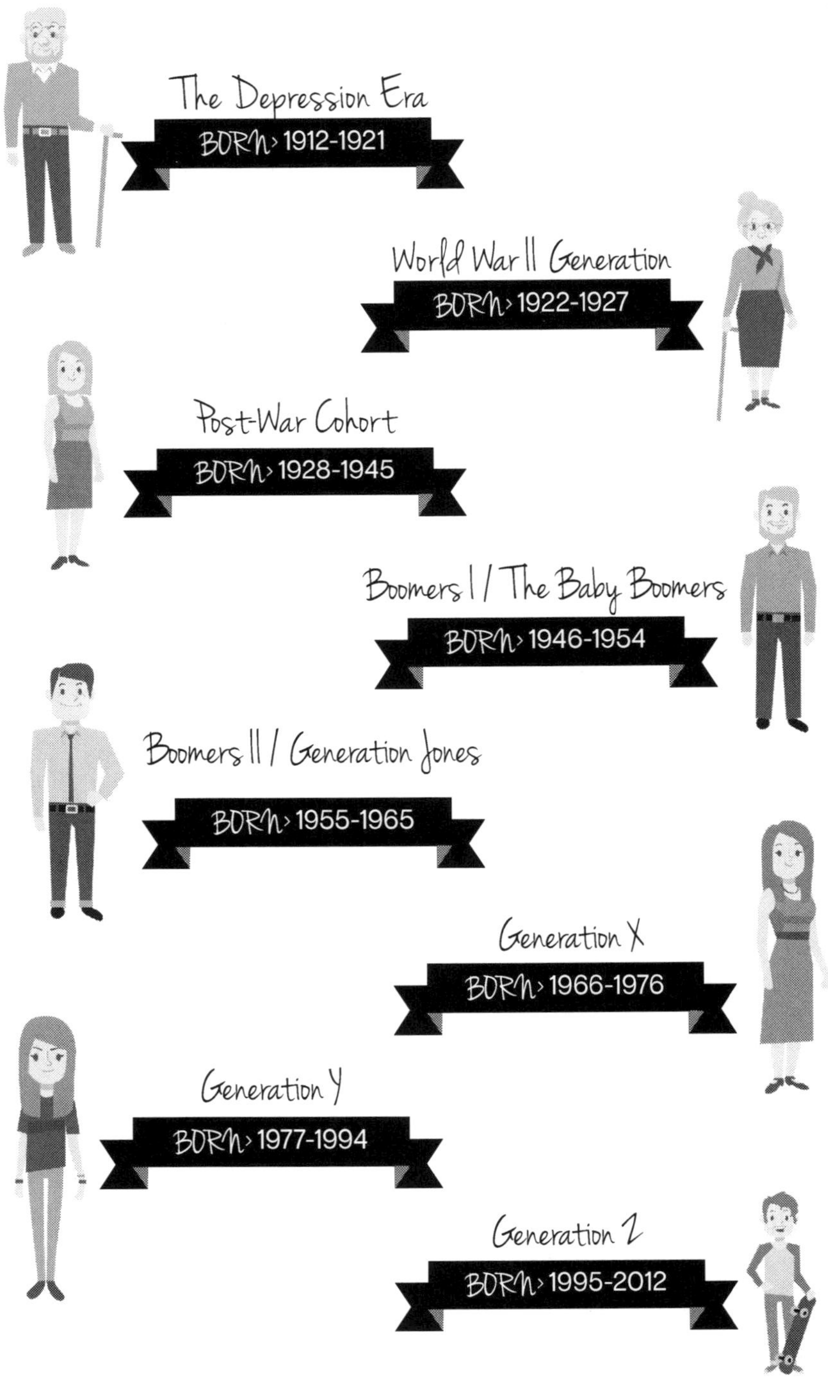
The Depression Era
BORN› 1912-1921
World War II Generation
BORN› 1922-1927
Post-War Cohort
BORN› 1928-1945
Boomers I / The Baby Boomers
BORN› 1946-1954
Boomers II / Generation Jones
BORN› 1955-1965
Generation X
BORN› 1966-1976
Generation Y
BORN› 1977-1994
Generation Z
BORN› 1995-2012

According to a study of Gen Z, "72 percent of high school students want to start their own business someday. Many of them are not even going to wait until they finish their education. Many of them are already taking up opportunities to earn their own money".[9]

In the Centre for Generational Kinetics, 2017 *Generation Y Study*, they discovered that, "77 percent of Gen Z (people ages 14 to 21) currently earns their own spending money through freelance work, a part time job, or earned allowance" and "nearly half of Gen Z, 44 percent say they would be most excited to apply for a job with a flexible work schedule".[10]

According to this research, the future of the network marketing industry lies in the hands of people who want to:

- start their own businesses
- have flexible work
- make a difference in the world

Gen Z also has some strong views about spending money. Studies discovered that 48 percent of Gen Z say they often or always get input from friends and family before making a purchase. This is a trait that is also seen in Gen Y where, "44 percent say they often, or always get the opinion of friends or family before making a purchase".[10]

While Gen Z remain quite young in their consumer habits, there appears to be a strong desire for this new age of consumers to get recommendations for their purchases from someone they know, like and trust. This is another exciting development for our industry if we are ready to harness it.

Conscious Capitalism

It is not only the Gen Zs who want to change the world. I believe one of the biggest movements we are going to see in business during the coming years is a movement towards Conscious Capitalism. There is a growing trend that business should be used as a force for good.

The original premise about caring for our world has always been as follows. Companies earned money, they paid taxes to the government and the government used those taxes to look after the people and the planet. Sadly, during recent decades it appears that our governments are not equipped, nor best placed to successfully fulfil this duty. With rising government debt estimated at around US$63 trillion worldwide in 2017, this resource is already looking very stretched.[11]

The second premise is that business in the pursuit of profit creates problems. Environmental problems such as pollution and social problems such as poor working conditions. When looking for solutions to the world's challenges we look to non-government organisations and philanthropy, alongside the government. However, these solutions don't have the capacity to scale up and quite frankly, the world's problems are now too big and too expensive for these types or organisations to solve them.

In 2013, Professor Michael Porter of Harvard Business School Professor demonstrated that the power that business has is far greater. He quoted that in the United States, governments accounted for US$3.1 trillion of monetary resource and non-profits for US$1.2 trillion. Corporations, however, accounted for US$20.1 trillion. He argues that not only does business have more resources, it also has the real ability to scale up.[12]

We need to re-align our thinking that the role of business is to solve problems alongside making a profit. This is not only an academic theory. Now many businesses globally are taking on these challenges and aligning themselves to not only make a profit, but also to making a difference. The premise is changing. Business is moving from being the problem to being the solution.

You could argue that the world has always had problems, so why is this relevant now? As we learned earlier, the world is more connected than it has ever been. Problems that once were far away are now right in front of us on our screens.

During his presidency, Barack Obama was acutely aware of this, saying, "The truth of the matter is that the world has always been messy. In part, we're noticing now because of social media and our capacity to see in intimate detail the hardships that people are going through".[13]

We are connected with the world around us and most people aren't con-

Professor Michael Porter, Harvard Business School, 2013

tent simply sitting there watching. Now people want to make a difference.

Many businesses are taking up this challenge and starting to focus their business on 'The Triple Bottom Line' of people, planet and profit.[14] Rather than simply assessing their business in terms of how much money they make, they are also considering the impact they're having on the environment and society. Interestingly, many of the companies that are doing this report significant competitive advantage. They are also engaging with their customers, and connecting to them in a much more meaningful way.

Blake Mycoskie of TOMS shoes, the founder of one of these companies, explains that, "Conscious Capitalism is about more than simply making money - although it's about that too. It's about creating a successful business that also connects supporters to something that matters to them and that has a great impact on the world... People who tell the TOMS story are more than merely customers, they are our supporters... Supporters beat customers every time".[15]

The loyalty and connection that companies get from their supporters is proving a vital key to success in a world where there is such a grapple for people's attention.

The security of money

Sugata Mitra in his 2013 TED talk, *Build a School in the Cloud* talked about the problems with our education systems, which are stuck in the Victorian era. He explained how our education system was designed by the Victorians in the Industrial Revolution to produce people who operated the machines that were being developed. Children were effectively being groomed to be cogs in the Victorians' machines. Like most things the Victorians designed, the education system was so robust it hasn't broken. However, it is now operating in a world that has moved on significantly.[16] This is an education system that taught everyone who came through it the principles of a good old Industrial Revolution job. Go to your place of work, do what you are told, do a good day's graft, stay for a set number of hours and get a wage. Then go home, spend time with your family and come back the next day to do it again. This is an education system that taught us our beliefs about work and what a job should look like.

The world we live in today is very different from that of the Victorian days. The work place has changed and will continue to change beyond recognition. While working conditions and pay may have improved since Victorian times, the reassurance of job security has gone.

In 2017, Forbes Magazine publish an article titled, *Job Security is Disappearing.*[17] This is a theme that is echoed across the work place. Human Resources expert and CEO Liz Ryan said that, "...when her parents worked full time jobs, it was common for people to stay at one job for ten to twenty years or even longer. In 2017, it's rare to find someone with job security for three to five years".[18]

Alongside this, with the increased capabilities of technology, jobs are disappearing. Worldwide management consulting firm McKinsay and Company published a report in the same year discussing the changes that artificial intelligence and automation will make to the work place. They estimated that up to 30 percent of current work activities could be displaced by 2030, and if estimated at only 15 percent, that would still equate to the hours of 350 million fulltime equivalents.[19]

With the use of technology, jobs are not geographically bound any more. In fact, geographic boundaries only really have a place in politics, taxes and immigration control. In terms of business, they barely exist. If a company can find better value resources on the other side of the world, they have the technology to access them.

Financial empowerment agency, *The Balance,* reviewed the impact of outsourcing on the United States economy, saying, "The main negative effect of outsourcing is it increases United States unemployment. The 14 million outsourced jobs are almost double the 7.5 million unemployed Americans".[20]

Furthermore, many of the jobs that are left are also not the normal hours that we were taught to expect from our careers. For example, many normal working contracts are being replaced by zero hour contracts. These are jobs where the employee has no guarantee of actually getting any work. They have the advantage of flexibility, but very little security.

In the United Kingdom between 2015 and 2016, the number of zero hour contracts increased by 20 percent. They only accounted for 2.9 percent of the employed workforce, however, it is another trend in the way our working world manifests.[21]

Throw in a United States and European predicted pension crisis with a raft of other economic problems and you start to understand why so many people think that now might be a good time to explore earning extra money. But the key here is extra flexible money to build security. Not everyone is ready to pull away from their Victorian styled jobs, not yet at least.

In my experience, the premise of a career is deeply ingrained in most people's psychology, but...

> ...most people are scared. Their faith in the institutions around them is diminishing fast and they are starting to realise that they have to take matters into their own hands.

In the United States it is reported that only 30 percent of people have confidence in their government. In the United Kingdom, it was a slightly higher – but still unimpressive – at 41 percent.[22] More than ever people are starting to become open to looking at new ways to build financial security for themselves and their families.

Summary

There are so many changes happening in the world now. Many of these are driven by technology. We are seeing many big shifts:

» People are more connected than they have ever been, but they are also feeling more lonely.

» Through technology we are showing people the world, but not showing them how to actually access and connect with it.

» Gen Y are now flooding the work place and feel unfulfilled and frustrated.

» Hot on their heels, Gen Z want to change the world and start their own enterprises.

» There is a growing trend towards Conscious Capitalism where business steps up to fix the world's problems.

» The whole market place is going through a massive shift as job security disappears and new ways of flexible working emerge.

While several of these changes may make you feel uncomfortable, there is a huge amount of opportunity waiting to be released from these trends. As we will start to explore in the next chapters, with network marketing we are poised in a perfect storm between what we can offer and what people are looking for. We simply need the right approach and tools. In a world full of noise, shouting our message won't be enough to break through and be heard. What we need to do is to go deeper and start connecting.

[Chapter 4]
HOW NETWORK MARKETING ENGAGES

In the fable, *The Farmer and his Sons*, credited to the Greek fabulist Aesop, there is a story of a man on his death bed. The man shares with his beloved boys that they will find all his treasure hidden in the soil of his vineyard. On his passing, the boys set to work digging the soil. They believe they are digging for gold coins, digging for money, digging for their fortune.

They work hard - really hard - because they are united together by a common cause. They feel a sense of belonging because it is their dear father's gold they are searching for. At first, they do not find any coins. There is no gold or treasure. However, the fable tells us that, "...their thorough digging was so good for the vines that they yielded more grapes that year than ever before".[23] Not only did they make their fortune from the wine they sold, but as a result of their hard work they were also united and fulfilled.

This is the last fairy tale I share with you because now we are going to start talking realities. Now we are going to start digging the soil of network marketing, but not for gold coins.

This book opened with the promise of showing you how network marketing's focus on money is holding us back. We are now going to pull together what we have learned so far about our industry and society. In doing this, we are going to reveal what appears to be 'the magic ingredient' that the successful network marketers exude. The, 'je ne sais quoi' that you have probably been struggling to put your finger on. We are going to reveal why some people sit at the table of network marketing and feast while other people sit hungry.

The common unspoken motivators

I will never forget the moment when I finally worked out what motivated me. The moment that lead me to start decoding Connection Marketing. I sat at the large round boardroom table at our company Head Office. I had been invited by the CEO with a few other select distributors who had all been recognised as movers and shakers in the company. We had the fastest growing and most exciting businesses that were producing record growth.

The aim of the day had been to share ideas about how we could spread this growth faster and stronger through the whole network. By this point in my network marketing journey, I had received much recognition for my business's growth, so sitting around a table chatting with directors and other high achievers was not unusual territory for me, but this day was different.

Rather than getting stuck into business we decided to go round the table and give everyone a few minutes to introduce themselves and tell their story. I don't know why it happened on this day, but for the first time people didn't tell their fairy tale, they told their real story.

They shared what the business really meant to them. They shared how it had changed their lives in ways they could never have imagined. It was not only the words they said but the expressions they used. I sat there listening to these amazing stories of people who had overcome all sorts of challenges and who had made such a huge impact on their own and other people's lives.

Now, I'm a pretty tough cookie; you heard earlier how my father communicates with me! I stick to my stiff upper lip British roots and very rarely, if ever, get emotional in public. But there was something about listening to all these amazing stories that made me literally feel like my body was welling up with emotion.

By the time it got round to my turn to tell my story I couldn't hold it in any more. Trust me I tried, but I had this huge uncontrollable, emotional outpouring! Tears streamed as tissues flew across the table in my direction. I desperately, but rather unsuccessfully, tried to compose myself.

What was that emotion? It was connection. It was not the full Connection Marketing theory, but it was the start of my understanding of it. As I sat and looked as this diverse range of people round the table I felt like I really belonged. I belonged to this organisation.

I also felt a huge sense of fulfilment and satisfaction. By building my business I had become part of something greater than myself. I had become part of an organisation that was changing people's lives for the better. All the hard work I had put in suddenly felt overwhelmingly rewarding. Not only did I belong, but I could also make a difference. And more than anything, I felt connection. I physically felt that belonging and fulfilment. This feeling was far greater than anything that money could buy. In that moment, I knew that not only was this what motivated me, but if I could harness that connection and if I could teach other people to connect, then the possibilities were endless.

What network marketing gives us is a tool so powerful that we can create connection in many different ways. In a world of lonely and unfulfilled people we have something incredibly powerful to meet their voids and needs. Connection Marketing is about harnessing this as a tool that anyone can use to grow a business and make an impact.

I returned to my father, but now with a different question.

"Dad, do you know what drives you?"

He shifted and arched uncomfortably because that is not an easy question to honestly answer. What he described were all the aspects that made him feel belonging and fulfilment, including the feeling of working hard, a sense of achievement, seeing the impact on other people, and sharing his success with his employees and family. Ultimately, what drives him is the feeling of connection and the feeling that he is creating something greater than himself.

Engagement in network marketing

Although people may initially believe they are joining network marketing for riches, this is only one part of the story.

There are three needs that our industry solves and which make people engage with us. It does this by providing a way to:

» earn flexible money
» avoid loneliness
» reach fulfilment

Think about the huge range of people involved in network marketing. They are all from different backgrounds, different ages and different levels of experience. I can think of no other industry that attracts people from such a huge, varied spectrum of society. What is it that unites all these wonderfully different people? It is their desire to fulfil these three essential needs.

I have studied and examined hundreds of network marketers and this is the common thread. They may not admit it (or in some cases they may not realise it), but it is this unique combination that binds us all together.

Importantly, when you examine those people who have success in network marketing, they are the ones who are engaging in all three areas. When all these elements align the distributor feels connected, they feel valued, and above all they are willing to do the hard work it will take to build a successful business. With alignment, that hard work becomes so rewarding it stops feeling like work. This is where the fun really starts.

Take any successful leader in your business and if they are brave enough to open up, they will appreciate that this is what motivates them. In fact, they don't need to admit it. Simply observe them and their behaviour. They don't travel to all those late night team meetings because they enjoy motorway driving. They do it because they want to spend time with their teams. They don't stand on that stage at company conventions because they get a pay rise, they do it because they want to feel valued and feel they are making a difference. The combination of money, belonging and fulfilment is what keeps them working way beyond the earnings they need. It is what keeps them engaged.

Now ask yourself - be really honest - do you want belonging and fulfilment alongside flexible money? Phrased like that the answer is probably going to be 'yes', but let's dig a little deeper. Are you brave enough to admit that deep down you are lonely, and lacking fulfilment?

The word lonely has so many negative connotations. It summons up images of someone isolated in a dark room rocking in the corner. But let's not forget what we learnt in the last chapter. Most of society is lonely. Connected by technology, but lonely. Admitting you are lonely is simply admitting that you are... well... normal! As for fulfilment, yes, things might be going okay, you might be pretty happy, but again you wouldn't be unusual in wanting a little more security in your identity and self-worth.

This might feel uncomfortable addressing such stark issues, but I am a big believer that no one ever has a breakthrough in their comfort zone. I want to stretch you outside our fairy tale world of network marketing where everything is perfect and we are 'fantastic' all the time. When we really understand and connect with what motivates us we can start to really connect with other people.

In the following chapters we are going to learn not only how to understand these feelings, but how to harness them for our own and other people's benefit. The reassuring thing is that you can admit to feeling lonely and unfulfilled with no fear because you already have a remedy for it. You have a network marketing business. Through this book you will learn how engaging with these needs will result in your success. So, be brave. Start to ponder. How big is your need for flexible money, belonging and fulfilment?

Balance

"Everything in moderation" is one of my father's keys to success. I must have heard him repeat this hundreds of times through my childhood, normally when my siblings and I were about to launch into a sugar glut! But this really is an important key to success.

> Success in network marketing is not only about fulfilling all three of these key needs, it is also about having a balance.

It is easiest to see why this is important when we observe imbalance.

■ Too much need to belong

I am sure at your company conventions there are always people who turn up to every event but never appear to move their businesses forward. They are completely committed to the company but don't appear to get results. In fact, sometimes they don't appear to actually want the results. These people have an imbalance of the need for belonging.

There is nothing wrong with this. They play a very important part in our community and provide a great support to other members of the organisation. We welcome and encourage them. The problem comes when they get frustrated and want to start achieving results. This is when they have to adjust their balance.

■ Too much need for fulfilment

You may also have met some network marketers who are like little excitable puppies constantly looking for recognition and fulfilment. They are eager to tell you how well they are doing. How many people they have spoken to and what promotions they are likely to qualify for. They would love to be put on stage so they can share their knowledge. They love giving advice to new people.

We love their enthusiasm and again they are a very valuable part of our community. They really want to feel important and be recognised. While they may be getting results from their own personal activity, their need for fulfilment will be alienating prospects who might consider joining their team. Again, the balance is out and they struggle to find real success.

■ Too much need for money

Finally, you have the group of people who simply want the money and they want it now. Their sheer determination may get them early

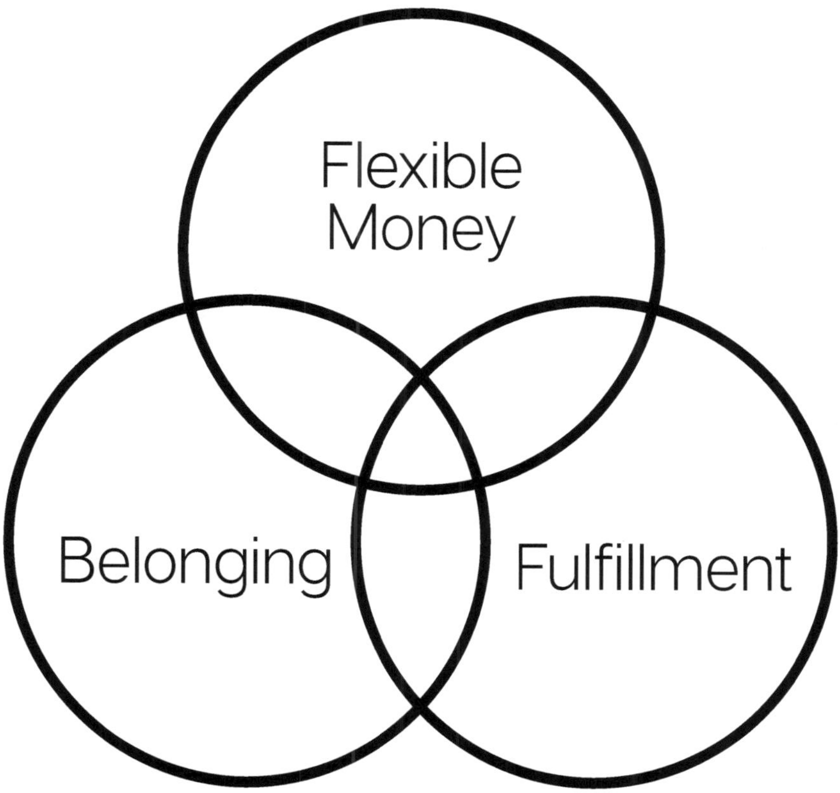
Flexible Money
Belonging
Fulfillment

results, but they will not have a long-term future in the business if this imbalance remains.

To be successful in network marketing you must have a real passion and desire to help other people to achieve. That is what makes us different from a normal sales role. I have often heard network marketers say 'sales people aren't usually very good at our business'. This is a bit of a fairy tale because there are hardcore sales people who have produced great results. In fact, we can be very grateful to these people because they often show us what is possible with determined focus. But generally, these results are in their personal activity and not in developing an active engaged team.

Of course, this is a generalisation and everyone is different, but a pattern I have seen repeated from money focused people, is that they make an exciting and quick start to their businesses. They often get good recognition along the way which temporarily makes them feel fulfilled, but unless they begin to engage in the sense of belonging and build a team, the recognition falls away and all they are left with is the money. At this point, their desire for money can get them distracted. It is more than likely they get frustrated with the work that has to be put into building a team and a solid business. It is not unusual to see these people get tempted away to a new network or the next 'shiny thing' that catches their eyes. These magpies will struggle to achieve long-term success until the balance is established.

You may recognise elements of yourself in the examples above. If you do, this is wonderful because it is a start to understanding where you are and how you can move forward. I have definitely recognised my imbalance both in the past and present. This consciousness will help you adjust and start to achieve greater results.

One word of caution; please never confuse what people say with how they behave.

There are many leaders in our business who often say that the reason they do network marketing is for the money. As we discussed in the previous chapter, this is because money was the currency that made sense when they were pioneering. I am sure if you observe how they behave, you will see they are being motivated in a much more balanced way. On the flip side, you may have people in your business who say they want to help other people, but given a chance they are first on stage to take the glory. If you are brave enough, you may notice how what you say is more what you 'think' you should say rather than how you really feel. This is another area we can work on together to edge closer to your success.

Changing imbalance into strengths

The great news about people who have too much of any of these needs is that they are engaged at some level. They may be frustrated that they are not getting the results they want, but at least they are connected and involved. If you have read this far you should have recognised elements of yourself in one or several of the categories above. This proves that you care and you want to be part of network marketing. The reason you have imbalance is because you have strength. Our aim will not be to water down the area that you are strongest in. Our aim will be to raise up the other needs to meet where you excel. That is why admitting where you have imbalance can be powerful.

If you have read this far convincing yourself you have the perfect balance, there is obviously something amiss. If you haven't tossed this book into the fire, I suggest you are brave enough to be searching for something. There are two reasons why people feel they have the perfect balance. Firstly, for whatever reason, you are not being completely honest with yourself. Secondly, you are not stretching yourself enough.

There have been times in recent years when from the outside it looked like everything in my life was perfect. To an extent even I believed that I had the perfect balance both inside and outside my business. I had a beautiful supportive family and a wonderful home. I had an income that gave me the choice to be present for my children's pre-school years. Alongside this, I had the engagement of a business that made me feel fulfilled. I had a brilliant team who felt like family and together we were achieving great results.

I had achieved all I dreamed of and more. I had made it and for a short time everything felt perfect... or did it really? If you had asked me, I couldn't have complained. However, the honest truth was that living the perfect life actually became a bit boring. That boredom turned into a feeling of being unsettled and unfulfilled. But how could I be so ungrateful? Many people looked up to me and envied me. If I wasn't truly happy with all this, would I ever be?

This was one of the most challenging realisations of my life, but also one of the most empowering. Up until that point, I had been looking at myself from the outside in. The evidence suggested I should be blissfully happy. But when I started looking from the inside out, this was not how I felt. When I finally began being honest with myself I took the biggest step forward.

I remember it being hugely uncomfortable, but I also remember choosing to embrace that discomfort. I remember trying to explain to my concerned mother that while I felt unsettled for the first time in years, I actually felt alive! Being honest with yourself is one of the most powerful things you can do.

As I discovered, the next step was to stretch myself. Don't compare your standards to other people. Even if you feel that compared to other people you have good balance. Even if you feel you are doing better than most people.

> You must stretch yourself. If you don't, you will end up feeling from the inside out that you have a life of mediocrity...

...even if on the outside it looks pretty good. Don't kid yourself and don't settle for what other people do.

If you don't have balance yet, this is the first thing we will address. Once you have balance in all three areas you will begin to feel connected. But the journey does not end there. You will learn that this is a never-ending cycle. I often talk about connection as currency is because it can be earned and there is no limit to the amount you can earn. You can become as rich as you choose in connection. You must keep stretching yourself. The more times you go around the connection cycle the richer you will become in so many ways.

To be successful in network marketing you must have a REAL passion and desire to help other people to achieve.

Part Two

THE WAY FORWARD

"The most deeply motivated people—not to mention those who are most productive and satisfied—hitch their desires to a cause larger than themselves.[28]*"*

—Daniel Pink

[Chapter 5] MOTIVATION FOR NETWORKING MARKETING

If network marketing is our vehicle, connection is our engine. Our engine has three cogs that work in unison with each other; flexible money, belonging and fulfilment. What we need now is the fuel for our engine. We need motivation. We understand why people want to engage in a network marketing business, but the next stage is to work out how to motivate ourselves and other people to do this. With the right injection of fuel we can achieve balance and progress. The challenge is that we have science working against us!

Scientifically lazy

In a 2015 experiment conducted by Current Biology, it was proven that humans are inherently lazy. The scientists equipped a range of different people with leg braces that added resistance to walking. They monitored the walkers on a treadmill. Very quickly they observed how the subjects adjusted their gait to reduce the amount of calories they were using.[24]

It is not only with physical tasks that this element is demonstrated. Social physiologists, Shelley Taylor and Susan Fiske in 1991, revealed the same results about the way people think and solve problems. They coined the phrase Cognitive Miser, discovering that humans automatically default to use the least amount of energy when it came to using their heads, as well as their bodies.[25]

Mandy Oaklander of *Time Magazine* concluded in 2015, "Humans are inherently lazy, which may be a trait left over from our ancestors' days of conserving energy for the next hunt".[26]

There are certain things that we all have to do in life, and when we don't do them there are immediate consequences. You can't get away with putting off picking the kids up from school until tomorrow, or telling your boss you will get back to their customers when you feel like it. There are things that we simply have to do.

However, the immediate consequences of not doing our network marketing businesses is that everything stays the same. Couple this with the fact that humans are inherently lazy, and we can understand why some people - in fact most people - never make an impact with their businesses.

Let's be realistic, building a network marketing business can be tough. It requires people to step out of their comfort zones, learn new skills and be incredibly self-motivated. The forces of human nature we are fighting against are so strong and ingrained in us that it is much easier to not have quite enough money and be a little bit lonely and unfulfilled.

We know we have an amazing vehicle to save us from this miserable plight, but now what we really need is the motivation to make us get up and do it! We need to fuel our engine of connection.

The fuel for our engine

In the bestselling book, *Drive,* Daniel Pink explained the three main motivators of people; autonomy, mastery and purpose:

- » Autonomy is the "desire to direct our own lives".
- » Mastery is "the urge to get better at something that matters".
- » Purpose is "the yearning to do what we do in the service of something larger than ourselves".[27]

Network marketing has to be the ultimate form of autonomy in the working world. We get all the amazing support that you expect as an employee, with all the freedom of being self-employed. While the corporate entity looks after the backend business functionality, the network marketer has complete autonomy to build their own business empires. Without motivation, this can of course be a bit of a double-edged sword. No one is going to force us and we are not accountable to anyone but ourselves, so we need more motivation.

Through the last evolution of our industry, the student days, we developed all the resources and systems for mastery. If you want to learn the skills of the industry and practice them to a level of mastery, there is nothing stopping you. Everything you need is readily available.

One of the most empowering parts of our industry is the importance we place on mastery. There are very few other movements in the world that so openly encourage personal development, sharing ideas and a supportive culture which believes a rising tide raises all ships. But we need more motivation for us to find the willingness to put the effort into this mastery.

I believe the biggest key to developing motivation in network marketing lies within purpose, or as I like to call it, a cause. Pink writes, "The most deeply motivated people - not to mention those who are most productive and satisfied - hitch their desires to a cause."[27]

Let's reflect once more on the image we have been projecting about network marketing during recent years; our royalty income story. It was quite a clever story because it appeals to our biology of laziness. If people were already 'lazy' then the only motivation in that story is the addition of money. Up until now the only real purpose or cause we have been pumping into our engines has been money.

Dan Ariely is a Professor of Psychology and Behavioural Economics at Duke University and a New York Times bestselling author. In his book *Payoffs*, he explored how money is not enough to be the sole motivator. He concluded that there are other motivators, which can be much more powerful. Ariely states that, "By focussing on that which gives us a sense of meaning and connection, we will not only stop destroying motivation, but we can start growing more of this incredible resource".[28]

To create meaning and connection we need a cause.

The power of a cause

Every business is about selling some sort of product or service. Let's imagine you are selling a product that no one actually needs, but if it is good enough some people will want to buy it from you. You are competing against many other people with similar products for the public's attention and sales. To make matters worse, every week everyone's sales results are published nationwide. Third party supporters will promote those highest in the league tables and help generate more sales for these people. There is much money riding on the success and sales of everyone's products. It's a constant battle to win people's attention and it is highly competitive. You are doing quite well. You have been on top of the table a few times and have many repeat customers.

Imagine that one day you telephone the people equal or above you in the league tables. You suggest creating one product together and giving away all the money that you make from it. Do you think any of your competitors would take you up on that offer? Almost definitely not! But what if there was a cause? A motivation that was greater than the money you and all your competitors could earn from the sales?

What if your name was Bob Geldof, your product was a pop song and your cause was starvation in Ethiopia. Then, of course this all makes complete sense. The story above is Bob Geldof's story. He was a reasonably successful musician with the Boomtown Rats, but only when he engaged with a powerful cause was he motivated to become spectacularly better than that.

The plight of starvation in the African continent spurred him on as far as organising the Live Aid concert in 1985, which generated US$150 million for famine relief.[29] The cause gave him the motivation to do more than his day job. While he did give away all the money from this venture it became a driving force, which motivated him to do much more than he had previously done.

Geldof engaged in a cause greater than himself and that spurred him on to do much more than merely maintaining his lifestyle. Although his motivation was to a worthy cause, this resulted in his profile being raised and subsequently his own personal value and wealth escalating way further than it would have otherwise. According to the Sunday Times *Rich List*, in 2017 Bob Geldof was worth an estimated £42 million.[30]

While this is an extreme example it demonstrates the real power of a cause. A strong cause motivates the person who believes in it, as well as engaging and connecting the other people around them. You may have joined network marketing to earn the extra money, but the real power of what we have is much greater.

Our businesses are actually vehicles to facilitate change. That can be small change, or it can be massive change. It depends how big a cause you choose. You may choose a cause that changes yours and your family's world. You may choose one that ripples out and starts changing the world of your friends and acquaintances. Or you may even choose one that goes as far as changing the world of people you have never met before.

The bigger the cause you connect with, the stronger your motivation. We are going to start helping you identify and engage your cause and empower you to grow it as your business grows. Through this you will create a sustainable business full of motivation that will be so exciting to build, you won't want to be sitting on the beach every day either!

What is a cause?

A cause is defined by *The Oxford English Dictionary* as, "A person or thing that gives rise to an action".[31] Something that motivates you to take action. When someone has a strong cause - as Bob Geldof proved - they will be more motivated than normal. For me, there are also four other criteria that make a cause:

1. It must be something greater than yourself.
2. It must connect you with other people.
3. It must do good.
4. It must be something you wholeheartedly believe in.

A cause can often be confused with a charity, but they are very different things. The definition of charity is, "The voluntary giving of help, typically in the form of money, to those in need".[32] Charity is about giving, a cause is about taking action.

One man's cause is another man's curse

Let me tell you the story of my friend Gary. When he was younger, he was one of those kids who got mixed up with the wrong crowd and got into trouble. He was a football fan and had gone a few times to watch a local semi-professional club playing. At the match, despite being underage he managed to buy alcohol with his friends and join a rowdy crowd of supporters. He ended up getting into a fight and being arrested.

Life wasn't going too well and his future prospects were not looking good. Luckily though, an organisation near his hometown set up a local community football team. They invited him along and distracted him from a misspent youth! He talks about how he learned many life lessons on the football pitch; how to work as a team, perseverance, winning and losing. His regular training sessions gave him focus and kept him out of trouble. He turned his life around and went on to be a respected and successful adult.

Later in life Gary went on to establish his own local community football team. This became a really strong cause for him. He had a powerful desire to give other young people the second chance he had experienced. He was willing to support it any way he could with his time, influence and money. The cause meets the four cause criteria I mentioned; it was greater than him, he connected with people, he was doing good, and he wholeheartedly believed in it.

One day, Gary was flicking through the newspapers and read an article which he was so disgusted by he posted it on social media. Where else would you express your disgust these days? An old man had passed away and left his fortune to a local semi-professional football club like the one where Gary felt he had been led astray as a youth. In his view, these clubs were the breeding ground for social unrest and trouble.

Although it was a completely different club in a completely different part of the country, Gary still couldn't understand why anyone would leave such a vast amount of money to this type an organisation. This was the epitome of what he cursed! Of course, this was only his opinion, but he was perplexed by the situation.

Compare that story to another that happened in 2015. It was reported in national newspapers that a recently deceased man, Colin Rowell,

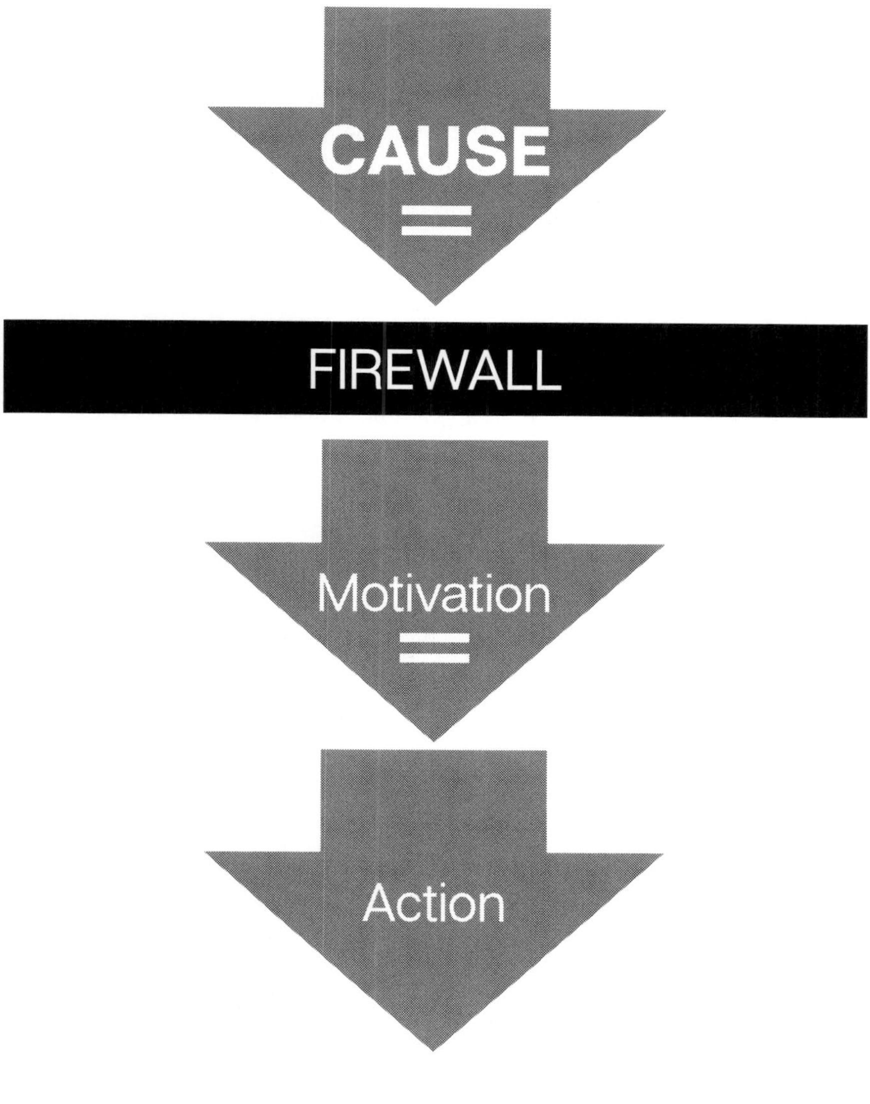

had left the majority of his estate to his local semi-professional football club. He had asked for his ashes to be scattered on the penalty spot of the club's home ground. His values and experiences had been quite different from Gary's. He had supported the club for more than seventy years and he had been attending matches ever since his father took him there as a toddler. He was emotionally connected to the club.

Supporting the club had become a very important part of his life. From the descriptions of how much it meant to him we can only imagine what a deep sense of belonging he had, especially in his older years. The reports talked about how much joy he had from his devotion to the club. It was something greater than himself. It connected him to other people. He felt a sense of belonging. He felt by bringing people together it did good. He wholeheartedly believed in the team and what it stood for. Rowell saw the club as a cause that brought people together and filled their lives with joy.[33]

Two very different perspectives, two very different causes. However, based on their individual values and experiences both were valid causes. If you had asked the two men to switch causes it is unlikely that either of them would have been particularly motivated. Finding a cause is very personal. If it is going to be a motivation for action, it has to connect deeply and meaningfully.

The cause equation

In the first chapter, we observed the reality of the hard work that it really takes to be successful in network marketing. We also talked about the frustration with lack of success. In an industry where we have all the systems and tools in place to support people, it can feel perplexing that there are not more people truly succeeding. Even more frustrating is that the largest group of people who come into the industry appear to give up before they have really got stuck into the hard work that is needed. I often see and hear network marketers say that what we need in our industry is for people 'to take massive action', but how?

I call this the cause equation.

Escape cause

Occasionally, we see the effect of this in our businesses. Normally it is when someone's life has got so bad they are confronted with a cause that suddenly motivates them. This type of cause I call an escape cause.

Several years ago, I noticed a lady in our organisation who appeared to be quietly, but deeply motivated. She got her head down and focused on building her business until she made a success of it. Only after a couple of years did the real reason become evident. She had been living with an abusive husband and escaping him had become her cause.

Protecting her two sons from him had given her all the motivation she needed to take action. Knowing that our business has afforded her the freedom not only to leave him, but to also take action against him, will always be a special feeling I will cherish. She had a really strong cause and used her business as a vehicle to change her world.

While the challenges in our world may seem quite grim for many people, normally they are not so bad that they become a big enough cause. The challenge with the cause equation is that the strength of the cause has to be big enough for it to break through the firewall to motivation.

One of the former network marketing strategies we have used was to go digging for people's pain. We tried to help them spiral into a chain of thought about all that is bad about their lives. We told people 'they need a why that makes them cry'. However, someone's pain needs to be so strong that they overcome their biological apathy.

In my experience, while life can be tough, there are very few people with an escape cause as strong as this team member's. There are very few people who have a pain so great they will be motivated to do whatever it takes and launch into massive action.

On the occasions that I have found someone with a really strong escape cause, it is likely that they need a lot more help and support than I am qualified to give. Alongside this, the emotional roller coaster that someone goes through in starting a network marketing business may not be a helpful addition.

The other challenge of this type of escape cause is that it creates less human connection. It is about getting away, not bringing together people. To that extent it becomes limited. Once someone has escaped, their cause has gone and once again they are left with no motivation. While it is wonderful to see them free of their pain it becomes very hard to motivate them to continue.

Why are you doing this business?

Often in network marketing we talk about 'finding your why', which is another way of encouraging you to understand what it is that motivates you. If you are not trying to escape from something, why else did you join the business? What is it that you wanted to change in your life? The problem is that most people who start network marketing find that their why is not strong enough to result in the action they need to succeed. I like to call this a stock why.

The stock why

As the contents of Julie's cup of tea flew across the table and she launched forward at me in a rage, I couldn't help but smile. This was the moment I had been waiting for! It might not sound like it, but this was the moment we connected.

An hour before I had popped in to see Julie. She had achieved success in our team and had the slow foundations of a nice business. But she was stuck. Through mastery she could now confidently gather customers, but she was struggling to build a team. Of those people who she did persuade - almost arm twist - into the business, very few got out of the starting blocks.

I asked her why she was doing the business.

As expected, she replied with her stock why answer, "A bit of extra money so I don't have to go back to work around the kids" she explained.

I smiled and said, "That's great, but I don't believe you".

She looked perplexed! She had asked me to come and teach her new skills and now I was sipping her tea and being... quite frankly, annoying!

"You see Julie, while that is a great story, I can tell that you don't believe it. There is no passion in your eyes, no fire in your belly, so really, why is it that you are doing this business?" I asked again.

She eventually admitted that she wanted fulfilment and to regain her lost identity when she gave up her career to care for her babies. However, building a business for the sake of earning more money was not enough. She needed a more powerful cause.

Julie actually knew the skills that she needed, but she was not motivated to perform them. Also, other people were not motivated to follow her. The problem was not skills, it was a lack of a cause. You will be pleased to hear that this was in the early days of my own mastery in helping people understand their cause. My support sessions did not usually end with broken teacups, but on this occasion I pushed Julie until she connected with the fact that there was more than merely money motivating her desire to do the business.

She eventually admitted that she wanted fulfilment and to regain her lost identity when she gave up her career to care for her babies. However, building a business for the sake of earning more money was not enough. She needed a more powerful cause.

Now I want to push you. Why do you do this business, and is that answer a stock why? Stock whys have a really important part to play in our business because they are a good tool for helping us explain our business to other people. However, what we need to understand is that these are often only our reason for joining, not our force for motivation.

What you need is a cause that is more powerful. A cause powerful enough to motivate you to take that massive action. A cause which will make you willingly want to do the hard work it takes to be successful in network marketing. A cause that makes that hard work so enjoyable, it stops feeling like work.

Connection cause

I believe that a much better strategy is to increase the strength of cause by engaging in something that will make people feel connected to the world around them. As we have learned so far, network marketing is the perfect remedy for so many of society's challenges. By providing connection we are perfectly placed to fill the voids that so many people are feeling.

We are poised to be the remedy for lack of secure flexible money, belonging and fulfilment. We are also ready to perfectly serve the next generation coming to the workforce. We have the perfect vehicle. But now we need to inject the fuel to get it moving. That fuel is a cause, but that cause needs to be strong enough to smash through the firewall.

We need to help people engage in a cause that is greater than themselves, so they feel part of something. We need to stretch their belief of what is possible and show them how powerful their business really can be.

[Chapter 6]
THE POWER OF A CAUSE

Arguably, one of the best leaders who ever lived was Nelson Mandela. He was a man who understood the importance of a cause to motivate and inspire action. Depicted in the blockbuster film *Invictus*, is the story of how Mandela engaged the captain of the fledgling South Africa Rugby team, Francoise Pienaar.

In 1994, Pienaar was already being criticised for his role as the leader of the disappointing Springbok team. He was under pressure and it appeared his cause was simply to maintain his role as captain. He had the skills to do the job but was not inspiring the action of other people. A year away from hosting the World Cup on home soil, the South African team were proving unable to win. They were barely a consideration to contend the cup in twelve months' time.

That is when Mandela stepped in. He met with Pienaar and at first appeared to encourage him to engage with his team and understand their collective cause. This helped, but the real breakthrough came when Pienaar realised that the cause Mandela really wanted him to play for was that of a united South Africa.

In the wake of apartheid, Mandela's intention was to reach out an olive branch to the white Afrikaaners who had imprisoned him for twenty-seven years prior. He wanted to show his people that blacks and whites could live and work together. He wanted people to forgive - like he had forgiven - so together the nation could move forward. Rugby was seen as a white man's game and many people could not understand why Mandela was supporting it. But Pienaar understood.

Rugby became the unlikely vehicle to unite blacks and whites in a common cause. Mandela enabled Pienaar to believe that if South Africa won the World Cup it would help unite a damaged nation. It would make their country great and potentially change the lives of 43 million people.

Pienaar now had all the motivation he needed. His cause was so great it didn't take long to win the support of the rest of his team. They began to understand his motivations and they too wanted to be part of it. The cause was now worth so much more than merely the prize of the World Cup.

In 1995, Pienaar's Springboks beat the odds and won the World Cup. They found the motivation and action to do what a year earlier had looked impossible. This is cited as one of the key moments in establishing Mandela as a leader of South Africa and helping break down the barriers that years of apartheid had caused. It united the nation and proved to be one of the catalysts for the country to begin moving forward, together.

With a game of rugby Pienaar and his team went on to change the world, because their cause was big enough. With a network marketing business what could you achieve?

Why you need a cause

■ Harness the power of your business

What if you are stuck in that trap where if you don't get motivated life will continue to be okay... but only okay. You'll survive with a few hardships.

> What if you are stuck in that trap of desperately wanting to succeed, but because of an imbalance in your motivations you are not getting the results?

My aspirations are that you will go on to choose your own cause and find your own way to change the world. Yes, change the world! That may sound grand, but we are going to explore the real power you have in your hands with your business.

This does not mean you will stop looking after your own needs first. It is vital that you come first. Understand this is a strategy to achieve your own success. I believe the richer you are personally – in every way – the more good you can do in the world. Success starts at home and grows from there.

In Chapter 3 we introduced the world of Conscious Capitalism. We discussed how business, in the pursuit of profits, has been seen as the creator of social and environmental problems. However, opinions are now shifting and people are seeing business as the solution. Therefore, you as a network marketing business owner can also become part of that solution, and there are many advantages to this.

I believe that by focusing on your business as a tool of greater purpose and impact you can unlock a deep motivation. This is how you will break through the noise of the media and really connect with people. This is how you will start to attract people to your business.

Ultimate attraction

One of the reasons I find many people struggle to talk about their business to friends and family is because they know they are going to financially gain from it. Most people find the thought of earning from loved ones excruciatingly uncomfortable. Even if we know our products or services will help, the fact that we also benefit makes our motivation appear disingenuous and almost unethical. Our friends also hate being sold to. They are fed up with all the noise in the market. Receiving yet more sales messages from friends or family often makes prospective customers put up their guard.

One technique we introduced into the team several years ago was to tell our friends and family our stock whys at the start of the appointment. The process of being transparent about our earnings helped gain trust and support. We saw an uplift in results, but in recent years this appears to have lost its edge. It also never took away a large portion of the discomfort that many distributors felt in an appointment and presentation.

Things change when you have a bigger cause. Imagine how you would feel if one of your friends approached you to sell you a product so they could retire early on £5,000 a month. Now, compare that to how you would feel about a friend who told you they were passionate about reducing the amount of homeless people in your town. While they appreciated it as a big problem, they had found a business where they could earn the extra money and free up time to help with this cause. Through that business they were learning new skills and were connected with a really supportive community. The people of this community were going to help them achieve their own personal goals, as well as progress this important cause.

Their passion and commitment to the cause would have cut through all the noise and now their friends and family will be listening. Not only will they be listening, they will have respect for the network marketer. When you have a 'change the world cause' something very special happens. It is not only you who is more motivated to take action, the people around you are more motivated to listen... and often join you too.

Having a business opportunity is one of the key fundamentals that make us different from a normal sales operation. As well as selling, we must also recruit and retain great people who align with our values. Bob Willard, in his book *The Sustainable Advantage*, explored the advantages of companies who hinge their business to a cause.

The top three reasons include:

» easier hiring of the best talent
» higher retention
» increased employee productivity[34]

When you start talking about your cause, people won't only be listening they will also be drawn to join.

> Everyone wants to be part of something greater than themselves.

They too are searching for belonging and fulfilment. Even if your prospect is not driven by your cause, they will see the greater potential of what you are doing and will want to be part of that.

Once I started talking about my cause I tangibly felt the difference in how people reacted to me. I often met people at networking events who thought they "had heard it all before from network marketers". They were uninterested in my business until they heard about my purpose.

They loved the story and once they understood my business was the vehicle that was helping me to achieve this cause, they listened more openly to what I had to offer. Having a cause at the centre of your business will motivate you, enable people to trust you and become a strong force for people wanting to join you in your business.

Why my Dad won't 'get it'

If you are reading this and are not convinced, perhaps it is because our perspectives are different. Perhaps you are thinking, "What people really need is security for themselves. They need that first before they can think of other people". Let's understand why there can be such differences of opinion.

I wouldn't expect my father to understand how powerful a cause can be, or for the pioneers of our industry to 'get it' because their perspectives are different from today's younger citizens. My father's generation grew up in a post war era where times were tough and people were used to literally fighting for survival. He was influenced by a generation who endured a World War and saw more than 60 million young men and women slaughtered. In his impressionable youth, people were in survival mode. People remember rationing. Charity had to start at home. Network marketing has served this need incredibly well, but now the atmosphere is changing.

In contrast, the younger Gens Y and Z statistically have had a life of peace. Mark Roser and his team from the University of Oxford produced statistics in 2017 showing the number of deaths from wars across the world. This data points to a long period of relative peace. "The absolute number of war deaths has been declining since 1946. In some years, in the early post-war era, around half a million people died in wars; in contrast in 2007, the number of all war deaths was down to 22,139".[35]

What about natural disasters? Roser's statistics show that the number

> *"Connected via myriad social media platforms and mobile devices, this generation has been able to SEE and SHARE experiences of troubles and unrest in REAL TIME creating a 'glocal' sense of shared struggle with their peers around the world.[37]"*
>
> —Afdhel Aziz and Bobby Jones

of natural disasters is significantly higher in the start of the 21st Century than it was at the end of the 20th Century. However, the number of deaths from these disasters is a tiny percentage of what they had been for my father's generation.[36]

Statistically, it might have been a peaceful time for humanity, but it has not felt like it. "Connected via myriad social media platforms and mobile device s, this generation has been able to see and share experiences of troubles and unrest in real time creating a 'glocal' sense of shared struggle with their peers around the world."[37]

Gens Y and Z have watched and shared the pain of these events even though they have not physically and directly affected them. Relative peace has felt like never-ending disaster. They have witnessed all sorts of tragedy in all-encompassing detail. With technology connecting the world, these generations "are experiencing a unique confluence of empathy and empowerment... they are seizing the opportunity to do something about it".[38]

This difference of perspectives is why the old premise - that network marketing was all about money - has got to be replaced with the premise that our businesses are a force for good, and a force to change the world. To attract, engage and future-proof our businesses, we need to change what we stand for and move forward with distributors who are connected and engaged with causes. Causes which they are emotionally connected to and which will motivate them way beyond what money on its own can.

Cause pitfalls

■ Never fake it

When you approach your business from solid, purpose-driven ethics, people start to trust you. Network marketing, to some extent, is a sales business. The public don't trust salespeople any more. By engaging a cause we show we are not merely salespeople. We are much more, but to build a relationship on trust it must be based on honesty and authenticity.

You can't fake the passion for a cause. You will get found out and then it will have completely the opposite effect. That doesn't mean you can't be passionate about someone else's cause or the industry cause, but your connection to it must be real. Having a cause is not merely something you tag onto your business. When you find one that is strong enough it becomes part of you, part of the way you live and part of your future.

■ Lara's paradox

I first met Lara in a shack of a guesthouse outside one of the townships in rural South Africa. I was exploring the area in search of suitable aid projects for my cause. She was also English and had heard that another white lady was in the region. This was a rare occurrence in this part of South Africa, so she hitched a ride along miles of bumpy roads to come and meet me.

Sharing stodgy maize pulp, she told me her story of how she had left her life in England behind a decade before. She'd had a spiritual calling to help those less fortunate than herself. She gave up everything and moved to the area. It was a wonderful heart-warming story, but as I began to dig a little deeper it became clear that all was not well.

In the early days of her time in the country she had managed to do some good, even if it sounded a little misguided. But as time went past life became more difficult for her. In giving up her job and her life in the United Kingdom, she had now spent all her money and had no source of income. She couldn't afford a flight to leave the country, her visa had run out, and she was desperately looking for work. As we spoke she was contemplating taking a job from one of the locals she had originally come to help. She felt she had to do this to survive. Lara had wanted to help, but now she had become part of the problem herself.

In finding your cause it is imperative that you don't become a martyr to it. Your business is the most powerful tool to help you fulfil your cause and you must never forget that. Remember that your business is the vehicle and the cause is your fuel. Without the vehicle, the fuel is not going to get you anywhere. Your business must be the driving force at the heart of your cause.

When you find the right cause you are going to be incredibly passionate and motivated by it. Make sure you always link it back to your business. While you will want to put time and effort into research and finding ways to meet your cause, this must not be mistaken for building your business. Your cause must not become a distraction. It must always maintain the driving force for more activity.

■ Barely surviving

But what if you are barely surviving? What if times are tough and right now you need to make sure you and your family get by. It might sound ludicrous to be thinking of other people at a time like this. However, having a cause is a very important strategy. Yes, your first priority must be you. You must first secure the physiological and safety needs for you and your family. But while you are doing this you can still aim high and think big. Thinking big comes with two big impacts.

Firstly, the small problems that are holding you back start to feel less significant. I have seen this effect several times. Team members who have struggled to pay their food bills have taken a step back to think of something greater than themselves. Afterwards, when they reflect on their own lives, they see them from a different perspective. They can suddenly see how the small things were holding them back.

These small things that felt insurmountable when they were focused on their own survival, now feel less significant. With this new perspective and higher purpose, they now have the motivation to do what it takes. They build their business and become successful firstly, for themselves and secondly, for other people.

The second big impact is how the outside world views you. Let us not kid ourselves. Most people are consumed in their own problems. They are blinkered by their own reality. Surrounded by other people who complain as they sleepwalk their way through life. Then you come along. You have a cause that you are visually passionate about and start sharing that story. Even if it is going to take you a long time to get yourself securely on your feet again, you are still working your way towards something bigger for the future.

You are different from most people out there and people want to know what this tangible energy is that you have. You tell the story of your cause and people find it refreshing. They get lost in your enthusiasm. You are seen as someone doing good and therefore, someone who can be trusted. Now people want to know about your business. Suddenly the outside world views you as different, as exciting, not as simply another person with the usual problems. The outside world wants to hear what you have to say and some people want to become part of it.

So, don't worry if you need the success of network marketing before you can actually help other people, but make this part of your journey.

[Chapter 7]
UNEARTHING A CAUSE

Finding your cause is not something that you are going to decide in the next hour. It is also not something that you discover at all; it's more something that you uncover. Thought leader Simon Sinek advises that, "It is a process of discovery, not invention".[39] The cause that will get you really motivated will relate to something in your past, one of your experiences or influences, which make you who you are. We are going to start the thought process to help you begin to uncover your cause in this chapter.

Types of causes

There are three main types of cause that you can get connected to. As you go up the levels, the power of your cause increases. Power in terms of motivation and connection to yourself and other people.

- » LEVEL 1 - Industry and company cause
- » LEVEL 2 - Team cause
- » LEVEL 3 - Your higher purpose cause

I appreciate this may be a new concept, so we will start with what you already have in your business and work up from there. My aspirations are to stretch you to think big - really big - and eventually get to the place where you can choose a cause so strong that you smash through the firewall to motivation with gusto.

Once you have digested this book, if you are ready for a higher purpose cause then get stuck in! Make sure you have a good appreciation for the other causes along the way. Alternatively, work your way up the levels. There are no right or wrong answers to this. The proof is in the results of your network marketing business. If you are motivated and attracting people, then you are succeeding.

LEVEL 1–Industry and company cause

The network marketing industry in itself is a wonderful cause. It gives ordinary people from all backgrounds the opportunity to create their own legacy and their own financial freedom. It fulfils people and gives them a sense of belonging. It is committed to developing people so they can be happier and achieve more. It is a level playing field. Network marketing touches and changes people's lives in so many ways.

In my early years I used the cause of network marketing as my motivation. I passionately believed that network marketing can change people's lives and this kept me motivated. This is a different mindset from merely doing network marketing. What makes network marketing a cause is not simply the money, but also the belonging and fulfilment. It is about believing in it as a tool to change people's lives and to do good. You must believe in the industry as a cause, as a powerful vehicle waiting to be harnessed.

The cause criteria test

If we assess network marketing by the four criteria for a cause, let's see how it stacks up. The first two criteria it meets easily:

1. It is something greater than yourself.
2. It connects you with other people.

What makes network marketing different from other business is the team building element. This is all about connecting with people and building something bigger than you could build on your own. Bingo!

The third criteria is to do good and there is no doubt that any respectable network marketing company does a lot of good. It gives people a fair opportunity to earn an extra income among many other benefits.

What about the fourth criteria? It has to be something that you wholeheartedly believe in. Only you have the answer to that question. If you don't already, I can't make you believe, but I can share with you where to look for that belief.

Seeing is believing

"Mum, is Santa real?" Eek, that question which every parent dreads but knows will come one day. As my son looked up at me with his big blue eyes I couldn't work out if he had an informant or was simply curious. Always trying to have an honest relationship with my son, I responded, "What do you want to believe, my darling?" He pondered this question for an agonisingly long time, while I tried to compose myself for whatever questions came next.

"Well, I know that there are lots of fake ones in the shopping centres and things, but what I can't work out is that if he is real, how can he actually get around all the children? Even with magic there are millions of children and his sleigh would have to be so big and we normally put the fire on at Christmas, so how does he get down without being burned? But he must because we get lots of presents and...."

There was only one thing for it - we needed to go and find some evidence so he could make up his mind. I wasn't going to lie to him and I also wasn't going to shatter his joy. I booked the family tickets to go to Lapland that Christmas and along with the grandparents, we headed to Finland in search of Santa!

Ably assisted by a specialised Santa tour company we spent three wonderful days riding sleighs, building snowmen, interviewing elves and searching for Santa. Needless to say, on the last day the children found a bearded man in a red suit.

My son assessed the information he had gathered and chose to believe. I quite clearly gave him the choice about whether he wanted to believe or not. I was very careful to make sure I didn't give any false information and let him make up his own mind. On the journey home we talked about all he had seen. We discussed if they could have all been actors and weighed up the evidence. He chose to believe. The questions stopped and Christmas continued as always... for the time being at least!

You have a choice too. You can choose if you want to believe. You can go on your own journey of discovery to find the evidence you need. If you think you do believe in our industry, I challenge you to go deeper, to increase your connection to our industry so you become unshakable.

Ask yourself, do you believe, or do you need to go hunting? I could have told my son the story about some people hitching a reindeer ride and finding Santa in the woods. However, it is unlikely to have had the same impact as our seasonal adventure. You need to go hunting for your own evidence so you can really connect and feel engaged with the cause of network marketing and your company.

Your company cause

Most network marketing businesses are built around products or services offering significant benefits to their customers. However, it is easy to get distracted by the headline news. I have often noticed how most network marketers hinge their business beliefs on one or two main benefits. These main benefits will be important and will be creating the main identity of your company. However, if we want to truly connect with the company first, we need to dissect it and deeply understand all of the reasons why someone might want to become a customer or a business partner.

Early on in my business one of my mentors illustrated this to me incredibly well. He drew a picture of a stool with three legs. "Name three beliefs of our business?" he asked. As I named the signature highlight benefits, he wrote one on each leg. "Now what happens when you speak with one of your prospects and for whatever reason that benefit is not relevant to them?" He explained if that belief was now gone your stool only had two

Belief 1
Belief 2
Belief 3

legs and it would fall over. He was right. The remedy for this was to make sure your stool has as many legs as possible, so if a prospect took one of them away it would never fall over. He was talking about belief.

I left that coaching session and drew up my own list of customer benefits. Our company only provides a small handful of services, but within one sitting I had managed to compose a list of more than two hundred business benefits our customers received. I included everything, from the initial ease of delivery, to the award winning aftercare. I trawled the company website, read all the small print and other Terms and Conditions. My list kept growing. Now my stool had hundreds of legs and someone would have to attack it with a chainsaw to knock it over.

You might think that this list became a good marketing tool to show my prospects, but they never saw it. To this day I keep an updated list, but I never show it to anyone, not even people in our business. Why? It is not a selfish act. It is because the finished list is not what is important. It is the process of building the list that matters. With every benefit I added, my connection to the company grew. My belief grew.

I keep my list with me, and in those early days I used to look at it frequently to remind myself of what an amazing organisation I represented. Reviewing this became part of my pre-appointment ritual. If ever anyone sowed any seeds of doubt in my mind, I sat quietly for a few minutes with my list. I barely ever reached the end because by the time I was half way through I found myself fully recharged again.

Start writing your list. Think of every benefit that someone gains from becoming your customer. Make another list about being a business partner with your network. Don't limit yourself to the benefits of the actual products and opportunity. What benefits do they get from the way your company delivers their customer services or from you being the introducer? What does your company do well or differently from other businesses? Are there any other future benefits they may get after becoming a customer, or perhaps pains they may avoid? Be specific with your detail. Don't make sweeping statements such as, "They will feel better" - dig deeper - how will they feel better? Why will they feel better? What impact is this improvement going to have on them?

While it must be your own list that you physically write or type yourself there is nothing to stop you doing this with your team or other buddies in the business. If you are going to do this properly you will need at least a good hour. Why not get a few of your network friends round for an evening and share a meal together while you build your lists. You can of course share with each other your findings, but make sure everyone produces their own personalised list encompassing all the benefits that the group discovers.

Am I in the right network?

One occasional error I sometimes see in network marketing is people switching from one network to another. Often they switch when they find they are not succeeding and go looking for the greener grass. This is a terrible strategy. While there are differences between each company, the fundamental principles are the same. They all buy into the same cause, which is people.

It doesn't matter what product or service your company sells, it is about the people who promote it. If you are satisfied that your network is ethical, you like the products, it has a reasonable compensation plan, and the company is committed to its distributor network, there should be no need to switch to another. This is all about people who use their business as a vehicle to change their world. It doesn't matter if that vehicle is a BMW or Mercedes. As long as you can drive it, you can follow the road to success if you choose to.

Cause enough?

Believing what you do in your business meets the four connection criteria is a really important starting point. You must feel you are part of something greater than yourself, connect with people through your business, have faith that it is doing good and have complete belief in it. This will give you a real sense of connection to your business. Although, I don't believe that is enough. I have met many aspiring network marketers who passionately believe in their company and the industry, but they are not getting results. They are fully connected to the cause, but going nowhere with it.

This is the foundation of your building. Like any structure those foundations need to be strong and stable. Without those foundations whatever you build on top is likely to crumble under any pressure. So, congratulate yourself that you have started your Connection Marketing journey, but this is only the beginning. Now you need a cause that is going to smash through that firewall so powerfully you won't believe there was ever one there.

NOTE: To mix it up a bit we will look at Level 2 *after* Level 3!

> "*Start at the beginning with the end in mind!*[40]"
>
> —Stephen Covey

LEVEL 3–Your higher purpose cause

Where the real motivation and attraction of a cause lies is in something so big that it changes the world. Occasionally, when I tell people their network marketing business is a tool to change the world they give me 'that look'. The look of, "I am not sure if you are deluded or onto something here". Sometimes they think, "that would be nice, but not little me, I only joined for the extra cash, I won't be able to do anything that important". Their head is full of doubts. Is this part-time little business really that powerful? I am here to tell you, "Yes, it is!" and that is where the real fun and success lies.

Your real value

Our first task is to find out what is important to you. We need to understand your values. When I used to hear the term values my instant reaction was one of disinterest. It conjured up images of corporate away days in my earlier career, when we spent a day working out what we thought our team should stand for and select a list of words to represent this. The next day everyone had forgotten our chosen inspirational words and we went back to how we all behaved a few days before! I can reassure you these values are not the ones I am suggesting we select here.

What we need is something much more powerful.

Values are defined as, "Principles or standards of behaviour; one's judgement of what is important in life".[41] Finding what is important to us is a vital part of finding our cause. When we have a clear defined image of this, it is much easier to mould our businesses and steer them down the right roads to our chosen destination.

Like my company away days, the reason most people don't engage in their values is because they base them around social idealisms, not what is actually important to them. In *The Value Factor*, Dr John Demartini explains how most people choose values based on what they feel is a "socially acceptable way of thinking and behaving".[42] For example, they select values such as honesty, determination, and thoughtfulness. A social idealism is anything that you could put at the end of sentences that starts with I should, I must, I need, or I ought. For example, I should be trustworthy.

Demartini says that while these are nice behaviours to aspire to, "They don't reflect the true driving force that shapes your decisions, actions and feelings".[42] They are generally based on how you perceive the outside world is going to see you. It is that outside-in thinking rather than the inside-out thinking I discussed earlier. It is hard to connect with this type of value because it is more about what you perceive to be important to other people, rather than yourself.

Instead of social idealisms, what Dr Demartini teaches us is to identify our highest values. He encourages us by saying,

> "When you become aware of your own highest values and wholeheartedly pursue the goals that express them, your life will begin to embody the kind of fulfilment and inspiration experienced by history's extraordinary leaders and achievers."[42]

A highest value is anything you can put I love, I dream, I'm inspired, or I feel, in front of. For example, I love spending time with my family.

When I first joined network marketing my values were based on social idealisms. I thought the reason I was joining was to make enough money so I didn't have to go back to work for someone else after having my children. I thought what was important to me was being a stay-at-home-Mum and a domestic goddess! My values were along the lines of, I should care for my children, I should organise my home, and I must be dedicated to my family. As it turns out, this is what I thought I should be, based on my perception of where I thought I should sit in society.

Never once did I stop to consider if this was what I actually wanted. I had this image in my head of me standing in a spotless kitchen and baking gourmet home cooked meal, as my two angelic children played peacefully alongside me. Seriously... that is what I thought!

As it turns out I am not the best cook, my ironing is pretty shoddy and my children are better described as spirited! More to the point, even if I was good at these tasks I don't really enjoy them. Now, my values are very different. My family do form part of my values, but not in a domestic goddess way.

What I value now are meaningful connections through a sense of family. That is a very different value! I have other values based around business progression and the things I believe in. What do you love? What is most important to you? It might be blindingly obvious, but have you stopped and actually asked yourself what values you really want to drive the next chapters of your life?

Write a list of all the things you truly love and dream about, that inspire you and make you feel incredible. Look for patterns in what you write. Are there key things that link these together? Be creative and really engage in this process. When do you feel the most excitement and joy? Write a list and identify your top values. Aim to have three to five highest values.

Go to Dr Demartini's website where there is an online score card you can use to help identify your higher values. You answer a series of questions, which help you identify what is really important to you.

Once you have found what your highest values are, you need to watch for a cause that suits them. Aligned with your highest values, what could you do to change the world? Think big - the bigger the better! Don't hold back. Don't worry if you have no idea how to achieve it yet, simply make sure it is something that meets the four cause criteria:

[1]
It must be something *greater* than yourself.

[2]
It must *connect* you with other people.

[3]
It must do *good*.

[4]
It must be something you *wholeheartedly* believe in.

Many people instantly know their cause. They can quickly identify how they want to use their business as a force for good. Other people take longer. Once you have started this thought process you will be more aware of what influences you, so keep it present in your mind. You will know when you have found your cause because you will feel the motivation!

LEVEL 2–Team cause

Some people find the jump from nothing to a cause a quantum leap. My own journey took a significant period of time to achieve. There is a brilliant solution to plug the void while you find your own path. That solution is to find a cause as a team or to 'piggyback' with someone else's causes.

A 'piggyback' cause

Scott Harrison was a successful nightclub promoter in New York City. By his own admission he was morally and emotionally bankrupt. One day he decided things had to change. He gave up his flashy lifestyle, sold most of his belongings and boarded a hospital ship traveling to Liberia. The ship provided medical aid and assistance to this impoverished country. As a volunteer photojournalist for the charity he got to see the heart-breaking realities of these people's lives.

One thing that struck him was the lack of clean, safe drinking water. He learned that many illnesses and deaths were being caused by dirty water and he decided something had to be done.

On returning to New York, the only vehicle he had was nightclub promotion, so he threw a party. He charged all his friends US$20 to come along. Taking this money to Uganda he used it to build fresh water boreholes. On completion of the project, he sent back pictures and live Google map positioning to all his friends who had donated money, showing how much clean water was being pumped. They loved this. Scott's friends felt like they were part of something greater than themselves. They felt they had done something worthwhile. This was the beginning of charity:water, an organisation that has gone on to provide more than 7 million people with clean water across a ten year period.[43]

Other than its amazing achievements, what makes this charity so special? It is the way it enables other people to engage in its cause. People not only donate money, but they feel connected to the cause. Supporters can follow the progress of their well being drilled, see images of the end product, and watch how much water is being pumped through their well on a daily basis. Hundreds of thousands of people have 'piggybacked' onto Scott's cause.

Not everyone wants to lead. Some people want to be shown the way to making an impact on the world. If you have not uncovered your personal cause, keep searching. In the meantime, why not find someone else with a cause you can get motivated and passionate about? Make sure you feel emotionally connected to it and check it fulfils the four cause criteria for you.

Why not also create a cause for your team or a group of distributors in your business? Work together to identify a cause you can all get passionate about. This can be a great way to get the sense of belonging and camaraderie. Finding a team cause is really powerful. It is a great way to help introduce new business partners into a purpose-driven business. You can really demonstrate how network marketing is a force for greater good.

Make your cause and your business come to life

Now we have the fuel of motivation in our engine, next we need to get moving. We need the cogs to turn. Cause is one of the 4Cs of Connection. The other three are Culture, Commit and Communicate. In the following chapters, we are going to talk about how you make a cause come to life by engaging with the other three Cs of connection.

Part Three

TAKE ACTION

The 4 Cs of Connection

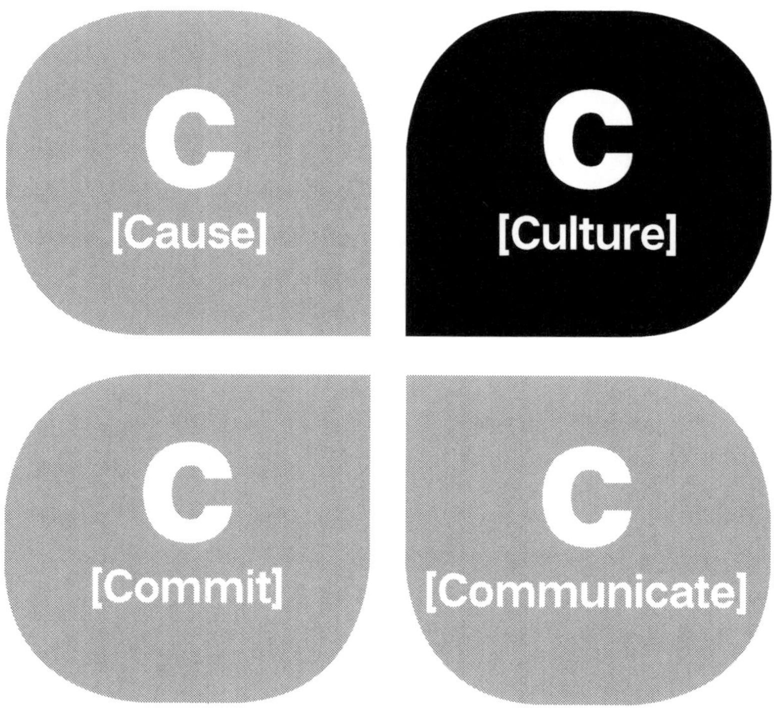

[Chapter 8]
CULTURE

"I never thought it would come to this", I sighed, as I looked down at the signature white stains on the shoulders of my top. My stretched and misshapen jeans weren't looking much better either. Long gone were the days of power dressing and carrying a smart leather satchel. These days it was all about an overflowing 'changing bag' rammed with emergency clothes, organic snacks and enough nappies to last a good forty-eight hours! Couple that with a pram to take the weight of the bag and of course, not to forget the actual baby!

If you had told me six months before that this is how I would be going to business appointments I would not have believed you. In fact, I would have told you off for entertaining such a ludicrous notion. I would never be that unprofessional. This is a business and it should be conducted in a proper manner. Oh, how I had to eat my words and beliefs, when I tried to build a network marketing business with a baby!

The first time I prospected someone after the birth of my son, it was with a lovely Mum I met at a local church playgroup. We had a good chat and rather awkwardly I invited myself round to her house to show her our business. Back in those days I had the old network marketing messages in my head; the, "It doesn't matter how you do it, get in front of as many people as possible" message. Before I even arrived things were feeling a little awkward.

The evening of the appointment I rushed our little bedtime routine, bundled up my son, thrust him into his Daddy's arms, delivered a bottle of warm milk and stumbled out the door. Five minutes prior to leaving I had resurrected the resemblance of one of my formal appointment outfits and even found the little brown satchel!

Adjusting my jacket and to an extent my composure, I rang the lady's doorbell. As the door opened, I remember a prolonged few seconds of silence as we both looked at each other in complete shock. There I was, standing looking awkwardly formal and there she was, standing there wearing exactly the same ragged clothes she had been in a day ago, although this time slightly more stained and stretched! In hindsight, I don't know why I was naive enough to expect anything different. If I hadn't been rushing out I too would have been in a similar condition.

From the minute I arrived the atmosphere was awkward. This lovely relaxed Mum from the day before was now closed and cold. All the rapport had disappeared. She offered me a cup of tea as she balanced her baby on her hip and filled the kettle with one hand. Out came my presentation and I did my appointment pitch. I ignored the overtired wriggling baby and like a true professional continued moving through the presentation as slickly as possible.

However, after showing her all the amazing things our company could do for her she hadn't warmed up. Awkwardly, she thanked me for my time and suggested maybe we'd see each other next week at the church. As I walked out the door I wished the earth could have swallow me up.

Why was everything I had done so successfully before not working since having children? More importantly, how was I going to fix this? What was it that was actually wrong and how could I change it? The key lay in culture.

The importance of culture

Culture is something we feel and it is incredibly powerful. If used correctly, it can be a fantastic tool for really ingraining connection with ourselves and other people. If used incorrectly, it can alienate the people we want to connect with. Culture has a big impact on how you feel about a situation, a person or an organisation. While culture is often left to naturally evolve, it is something we can and should consciously mould. Creating a culture is like designing the personality of our business.

When you have a good culture that aligns with you and your cause, it will help you feel more comfortable in your business. Most importantly, it will help other people feel secure when they engage with you. As your cause grows and your business starts to impact more people the importance of your culture will become paramount. The process of designing a culture that fits what you are trying to achieve will help you create connection and success.

Many of the business success stories during the last decade have cited culture as one of their keys to success. For example, Zappos the American online retailer is seen as a world leader in creating culture. In 2009, they were thrust into the press when they sold to Amazon or 'became part of the Amazon family' as they like to describe it, for what is estimated at more than US$800 million.[44] A pretty impressive valuation for a company that had started ten years prior.

Tony Hsieh, the CEO of Zappos explained how, "Culture became our number one priority". Their strong culture was a lynch pin in their success.

> "At Zappos, our believe is that if you get the culture right, most of the other stuff—like great customer service, or building a great long-term brand, or passionate employees and customers—will happen naturally on its own."[45]

As network marketers, building a strong culture is almost more important for several reasons.

Firstly, when we are out in the field we are the face of our company and the face of our brand. We might have flashy presenters and great sample products, but what gives us the competitive edge is 'us'. Yes, you and I are much more powerful than a normal social media, televised or printed advertisement. We are out there as a living embodiment of the brand. As Heist explained, “Your culture is your brand”.[45] Therefore, we need strong personal culture.

We also need a strong culture in our teams. Our work force are effectively volunteers - and scattered volunteers at that. We don’t have hours each day to sit in an office together and we need to make our people feel part of something greater than themselves. Having a strong culture will help everyone feel connected and feel a sense of belonging.

It is also important for those people on the outside looking in. With the forces of social media there are always people watching. If they see a strong culture they like, they will be attracted to become part of it. Attracting people to choose to come and work with us is the lifeblood of our businesses. We need to not only have but live by a strong culture.

Be the crazy lady in the woods

I was recently travelling through South Africa and taken to visit a lady who had been described as ‘a crazy lady who lived in the woods and did spiritual readings’. I’ll be honest, I didn’t want to go. Our group had been travelling for several weeks and we had recently completed a mountain hike. We were tired, irritable and in all honesty, physic readings really aren’t my thing. Too polite to say no, we drove out to this woodland shack.

As I looked around at my fellow travellers their faces looked as pained as mine must have. Reluctantly, we walked into a small dark room, cluttered with books and knick-knacks. There were chairs laid out around a flip chart and a little old lady standing at the front who beckoned us to have a seat. We were going to be a tough crowd to please!

But something quite special happened. This thin, softly spoken lady started talking about her story and how she got into doing readings. As she did so, a tangible feeling of calmness came across our group; people relaxed and began to engage. Within minutes we had all fallen in love with this wonderful woman. What was it that she did to win over a group of irritable sceptics? It definitely was not the scatty, unplanned presentation. I am pretty sure there wasn’t any love incense burning either!

We ended up staying for the whole afternoon not only in her treatment room, but we were also welcomed into the lady's home. I sat on her sofa feeling completely inspired and began to understand her power. It was her authenticity. She really knew who she was and she was comfortable with that. She knew what her purpose was and she knew her strengths and her weaknesses. Everything about her culture and behaviour reflected that. She was fully connected with herself and that made everyone else feel secure and comfortable in her company.

This really illustrated to me the power of developing your own personal culture and being congruent with yourself. This is where we must all begin our culture journeys.

Personal culture

After my disastrous first appointment as a mother I sat down and redesigned my culture. I had tried to fit my new life into that of the 'perfect-career-Mum' image I had in my head, but it didn't work. It wasn't me and it didn't fit. I started to look around for inspiration from other career Mums. I expected to see perfectly manicured Mums sitting in front of laptops with a gorgeous clean baby who didn't consistently whack their chubby little wrists on the keypad.

It turned out that these women don't actually exist. Or, at least after a decade of searching I haven't been able to find them except in highly edited photo shoots. What I did see were plenty of other women like me. Women who had plenty of skills deeply buried in the routines of demanding little people. Women who appeared to have given up their identity and taken on a new culture as I had.

I started to be authentic to myself, to embrace personal culture and bring it into my business. Rather than doing appointments, I started doing play dates. Rather than building a team, I started building a family. Rather than power dressing, I Mummy dressed. Rather than the satchel, it was a changing bag!

The first appointment I did as a play date felt daunting. I was concerned how I would cope with the constant interruptions and if it would appear unprofessional. I shouldn't have worried. My baby cooed at the other lady's baby. We stopped several times to feed or rock our little ones and the whole atmosphere was very relaxed. Not only did the lady take all of our services but she was also fascinated by our business model.

She had witnessed me having a lovely morning with my baby, a cup of tea with a friend and helping someone out with our services. I explained to her that I got paid for doing this and I belonged to a group of other people like me. I was regaining my identity and it was giving me the choice not to return to work. We talked about her job. She was reluctantly going back after maternity leave and it didn't sound very appealing. Before I knew it, I had a new distributor in my team and the family started to grow.

Have a think about your personal culture. How do you look from the outside in and is this reflected authentically in how you feel from the inside out? Consider what you want your personal culture to stand for. How does that influence the way you dress, the way you conduct your presentations, the language you use and how you post on social media? Mould your culture to become an attractive force for the outside world.

Team culture

It wasn't only my appointments culture that changed. The team culture began altering to embrace these new Mums who were joining us and wanted a corporate escape route. Evening team meetings were pushed back to after bedtime. Often, we met with our little ones at local play centres during the day. We started running monthly presentations at local village halls. We bought a big play mat and toys. The babies played while we shared our opportunity with the Mums and occasionally, Dads too!

This strong culture saw our businesses grow and accelerate. Alongside the new Mums, other people became more interested. By demonstrating how the business could be moulded to my lifestyle, other people saw clearly how they too could mould it around their lives. The culture became less about what we actually did and more about how we did it.

Our culture was and continues to be about family. This family culture is based on a clear set of values. We treat each other like a loving supportive family. That means when times are tough we are there for each other.

When things are going well we celebrate with each other. We welcome new team members as we do a new family member. We even go as far as all shacking up together in hundred-bed youth hostels when it comes to big company events!

We have a team name, a team logo, private social media groups and when we get together, we normally have items of team apparel to visually pull us all together.

Understanding that our culture is based around family makes it easier to make decisions. If someone's results are lacking, we don't turn our back on them. If one of your children was struggling at school you wouldn't kick them out; you would do everything you could to help them. The same applies in our team.

Through having a strong team culture and identity not only do the team members feel a heightened sense of belonging but also, they feel safe. Network marketing can be scary. People must overcome their fears and step out of their comfort zone to be successful. We need to provide a culture where people feel safe to fall back on.

Simon Sinek explained how a strong culture creates a "circle of safety" around people that "reduces the threats people feel inside the group, which frees them up to focus more time and energy to protect the organisation from constant dangers outside and seize the big opportunities.... Only when we feel that we are in a circle of safety will we pull together as a unified team, better able to survive and thrive regardless of the conditions outside".[46]

As a team we chose a culture of family. You can choose a culture of whatever you feel fits and aligns with your group. What is important is that you make a conscious choice, not what the choice is. Consider your values, your team's values and what values you want to project to the outside world. Use this as a guide to mould yourselves and your team.

Cause culture

Once you have a cause in your team, your team culture will grow to support that. When we moved to being a cause-centric team we continued acting like a family, but enhanced this. In fact, by being a purpose-driven network marketing business we felt closer together and having causes became part of our culture. Collectively uniting in something greater than ourselves helped increase the sense of belonging and fulfilment in the team. Ironically, by looking at something bigger than the team, we all began to feel tighter and closer. Use your cause to enhance your team culture.

Misfit culture

It is highly likely when you have a strong culture you will attract likeminded people. They will be drawn to you because of your culture. However, occasionally people will join whose personal culture does not fit with the team. Perhaps you are in a team at the moment and you don't feel you quite fit.

If you have felt uncomfortable or frustrated with your upline and other team members, it is more than likely because of misfit culture. If you have someone in your team who appears disengaged and annoyed, they may also be misaligned. It is important that you try and identify this as soon as possible. There are actions you can take to remedy the situation.

Firstly, sit down with your upline or the new team member who is struggling and have a conversation about the team culture and why you feel it fits. It could be that the culture is not clearly defined enough and once it is clarified the uncomfortable distributor feels they can adapt and align to it. If it is a good healthy culture it is highly likely they will want to mould their personal culture to fit the team culture.

If this is unsuccessful, it may be a genuine misalignment, but not all hope is lost. Within your business there are other teams with other cultures. Help the distributor find a team which they feel is more aligned to them.

Always be willing to accept people from other teams to join your team if they align with your culture. People who seek you out because of culture will always add a huge amount of value to your team. With the right culture, while they may not be in your downline they will help support other people who are and enhance your business.

If you are a leader in your business, make sure you connect with other leaders including those with different styles and cultures. Build relationships even if your cultures don't align. While you might not see the world in the same way, if you have a strong relationship you will learn a vast amount from each other. Understand that sometimes you may not see eye to eye on the way that things are done, but by challenging each other you have an opportunity to grow. No one ever has a breakthrough in their comfort zone. You need people to challenge you.

Look out for different cultures and embrace them.

The 4 Cs of Connection

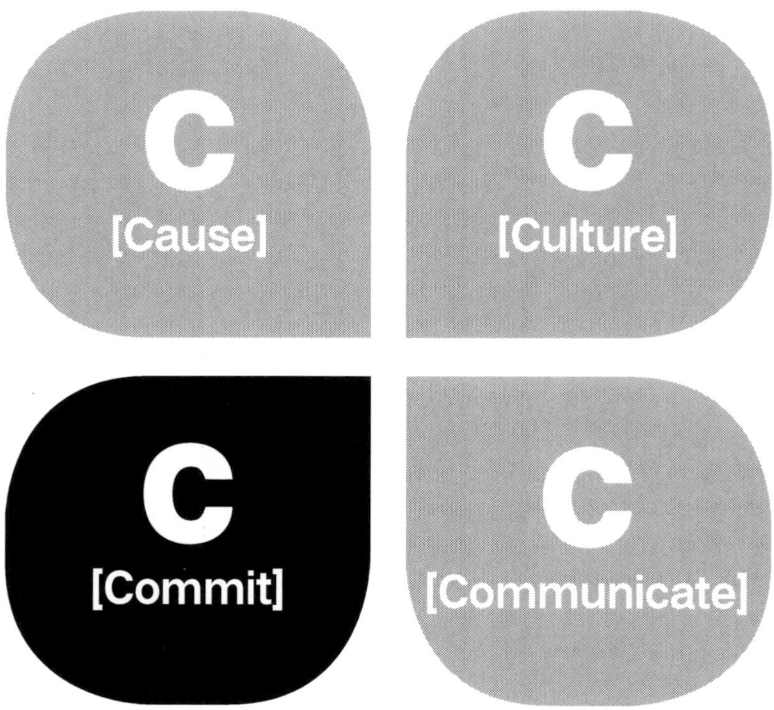

[Chapter 9]
COMMIT

As you feel the warm water trickle through your hands you notice your shoulders and back begin to ache. Almost mesmerised you watch the water washing the paint off the roller. It has been a long, hard day. There were times when you couldn't bear the thought of another coat of paint, but you kept going. The sound of the paint getting squelched and spread across the walls echoes in your ears. You finish cleaning your brushes and head back to look at your newly painted room.

You stand there gazing in admiration. You go and have a shower and come back to appreciate your handiwork once again. Despite the fumes of the drying paint you must go and check the room at least once more before you go to bed. The walls have not changed, they look exactly the same as they did an hour ago, but you can't help yourself returning time and time again.

If you have done home decorating you will recognise this feeling. It is a feeling of pride, fulfilment and satisfaction that comes from getting a job done. Even if you hate decorating, there is a feeling of reward from working hard and achieving something. When you commit to your network marketing business that feeling is waiting for you, but it doesn't go when the paint dries, it lingers on and on. It makes success in our businesses feel sweet.

The reality of hard work

If you have been at a network marketing event and seen people being recognised for their achievements they are often euphoric. In our company it is not unusual to see celebration dances, air fist pumps and on one occasion a lady hugged our company CEO with such gusto she lifted him off his feet!

The reason network marketers get so excited is because success in this industry is hard work. But it is the most rewarding work I have ever known. When you succeed in your business, you will not regret a second you have invested. But to succeed we need to be realistic. It is going to be intense and you need to commit.

Not all hard work is equal. Sometimes the simplest of tasks feels like hard work because you don't enjoy them. In contrast, very challenging situations can feel exciting and fun when you are engaged. To be successful in network marketing you need to commit time and effort. It is important that you find a way to make that immensely enjoyable.

Much enjoyment will come from working towards a cause that you are emotionally connected to; from working with likeminded people that you will find in our industry, and to the sense of belonging you will get from your team. However, you need to consciously commit to your business. Let's look at ways to enhance that commitment.

Happiness lies in commitment

Hard work is going to make us happy. We are going to get that amazing feeling when we succeed. Paul Dolan is a Professor of Behavioural Science and bestselling author of *Happiness by Design*. He identified that,

> "To be truly happy, then, you need to feel both pleasure and purpose."[47]

Harping back to where we started this book, that is why sitting on the beach does not make us happy. It is pleasurable, but there is no purpose. If we are able to commit to our businesses, we need to feel happy. We must achieve pleasure and purpose.

There will be many pleasures from your business. There will be friendships, recognition, belonging and of course rewards; both financial and other incentives. However, as we have previously explored, on their own these are often not enough to motivate us without a cause. To commit we need a cause and a purpose.

In his study of successful people with, *Grit,* the New York Times bestseller, Angela Duckworth revealed that, "the long days and evenings of toil, the setbacks, disappointments and struggle, the sacrifice - all this is worth it because, ultimately, their efforts pay dividends to other people".[48]

One of the lessons I learnt from my father was that if something was easy it wouldn't be worth doing anyway. Make the decision now to commit to the hard work ahead in the knowledge that for every struggle the reward will feel greater. Only by truly committing will the journey feel worthwhile. Without that commitment your success is on hold.

Sacrifice

"If you want to be successful in this business then forget about your kids, they won't remember you not being there for their little birthdays, but they will remember when you buy them a car when they turn 17". Less than ten years ago, that is what I was told. For the leader telling me this, that was true for him. As one of the great pioneers of our industry he had committed and sacrificed pretty much everything, and we should all be thankful to the men and women of our industry who gave so much to get it to where it is today.

However, things have changed and moved on. While there will be sacrifices and serious hard work, today's network marketers are incredibly privileged to be able to achieve balance in their commitment. My business became a tool to enable me to stay at home with my children and I did not miss a single moment of their pre-school years. I will also be able to buy them a car at seventeen, if I feel this is the right thing to do. Instead, I will choose to make other sacrifices. I have become much more deliberate about how I invest my time. I have also had to become much more organised.

If you are going to commit to network marketing, you have to invest time and effort in doing that. Human time is like a goldfish. If you put a goldfish in a bigger tank it proportionately grows to fill its larger home. If humans have spare time it will get filled. That is why everyone is always busy, it is pretty much impossible not to be busy! To find the time to invest and commit to your business you are going to need to sacrifice some things. When you remove something, you create a vacuum. If you don't consciously fill the void, something or someone else will.

While I have never had to sacrifice anything that was really important to me, I have consciously cut things out of my life. Very rarely do I watch television. I choose not to burden myself with the negativity of mainstream news and media. I have distanced myself from friendships with people who always appeared to be holding me back. Make a conscious choice about what is really important to you and what serves you no real purpose. Begin to create vacuums and consciously fill them with the activities that will drive you and your business forward.

Like me, you won't always get the balance right. At one point I found I was keeping myself so busy I forgot to care for my own health. I started struggling with several little ailments, which ultimately slowed me down. I had to readjust the balance and invest time in myself. Now, I am always adjusting and improving my focus. This is an activity that evolves as you do it.

Commit to the right mindset

Once you have identified time, you need to fill it. Firstly, you need to commit and invest in the right mindset. Leading Professor of Psychology, Dr Carol Dweck, identified two different types of mindset; fixed mindset and growth mindset. The fixed mindset believes, "that your qualities are set in stone" while the growth mindset, "is based on the belief that your basic qualities are things you can cultivate through your efforts".[49] To commit to network marketing you are going to need a growth mindset. There are many skills to learn to become successful and part of the hard work is to embrace stretching and changing yourself.

"People in a growth mindset don't just seek challenge, they thrive on it. The bigger the challenge, the more they stretch," says Dr Dweck.[49]

Being successful is about enjoying the hard work, thriving on the challenge of a cause and committing to it.

Ask yourself, how willing you are to change and learn? Are you willing to stretch yourself? To be successful you must commit. To be successful you will need to grow.

Commit to turning up

Going to company and team events is a vital part of your business. It is at these events that you really feel the emotional connection with your company. It is like a restaurant experience; reading the review about it in the papers is nowhere near as rewarding as tasting the food. You need to be there so you can experience the connection.

Events are also where you will build relationships with other distributors. I have met some of my closest friends at company events, people who have become the most supportive buddies within and outside the business. If I had turned up only once I would not have made these connections. Commit to becoming a familiar face. Commit to engaging with other people at the events.

However, if you only turn up, you are not getting the full value. Invest time before an event and get your team there. Invest in the effort while you are there to meet and connect with other distributors. Invest time afterwards putting into action what you learnt. If you simply go, have a nice day and don't make any changes you have lost the value.

Commit to mastery

In Chapter 4 we talked about the cause equation. A cause creates motivation, which creates action. But that is not the end of the story. To change that action to success we need to add mastery. We need to commit to learning the skills of our trade. Some of these are practical skills such as presenting, while others are softer skills such as building rapport.

We are incredibly fortunate that in our industry and within our companies we are surrounded with many amazing resources to help us edge towards mastery. In the book *Outliers*, author Malcolm Gladwell claimed that it takes roughly ten thousand hours of practice to achieve mastery in a field.[50] After a decade, I continue to have more to learn, but I am fully committed to investing in that learning. You will need to do the same. Commit to learning, changing and growing.

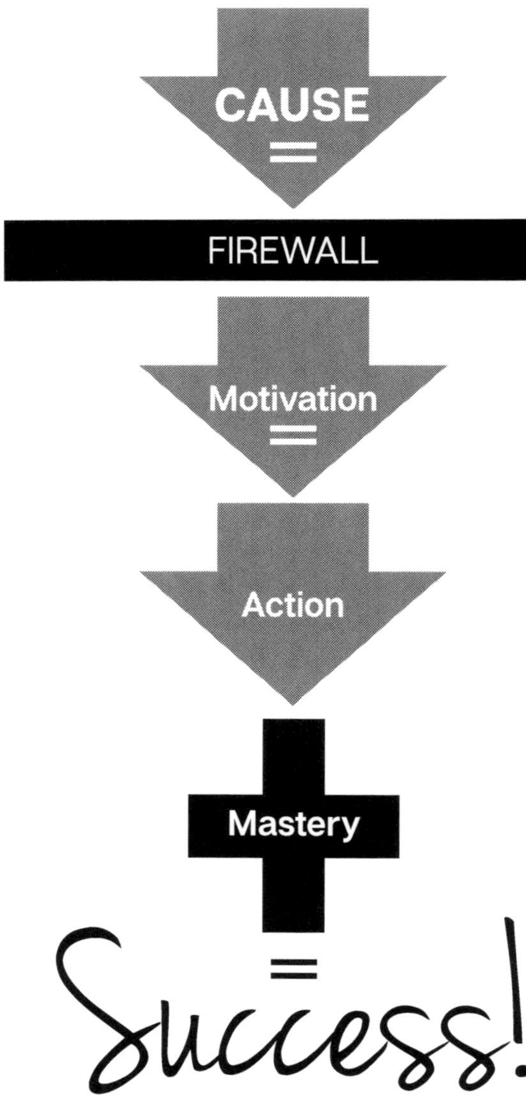

Commit to taking action

Ben Hunt-Davis is an Olympic gold medallist rower who we can learn much from. In his fascinating book he recounted the journey to medal success. The book's title alludes to the over-riding question the team asked themselves, *Will it Make the Boat Go Faster?*[51]

When working towards a big goal there are many things you can do to improve your performance and it is easy to get distracted by low payoff activities. The rowing team were very proactive, but they made sure they focused only on whatever made the boat go faster. In network marketing there are also many distractions. You need to learn which activities are going to make your boat go faster. You need to commit to taking action, but make sure it is the right action!

While you need to invest time in mastery, look at this as more of a hobby than a money making activity. You need to do it, but don't kid yourself it will actually build your business. I have seen many people fall into the trap of becoming training and personal development junkies. You will learn more from doing, reviewing and adjusting from real appointments with real people, than you will in a classroom or on a training portal. Learn the skills and get out there to master them in the field.

The ultimate commitment you need to make is speaking to people. It is about communication, which leads us nicely on to the last C of Connection.

The 4 Cs of Connection

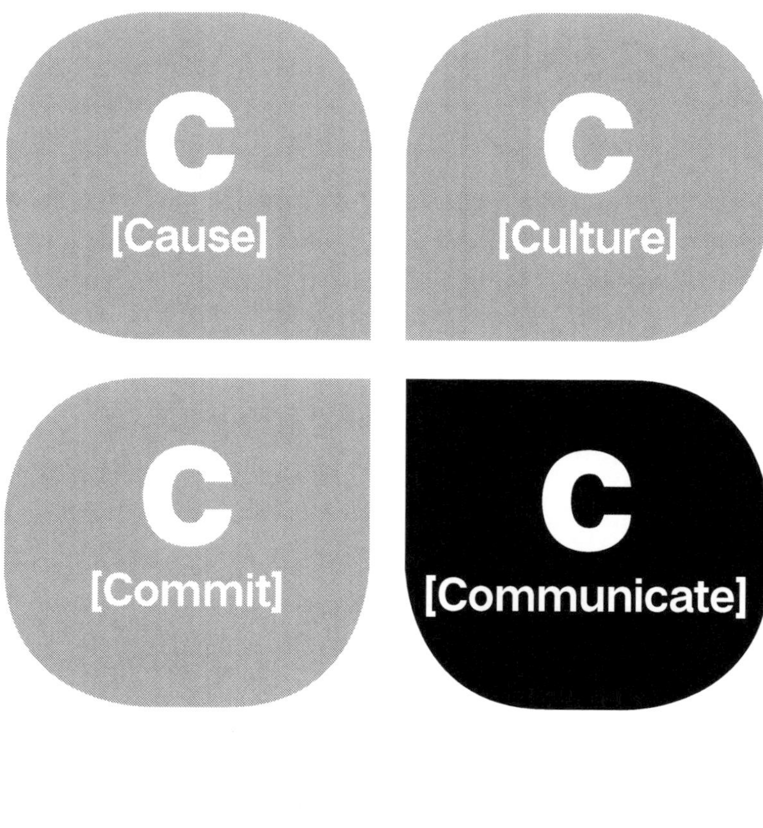

[Chapter 10] COMMUNICATE

"No way am I eating that!" my son protested.

"Ugh, what is it?" added my daughter.

Not the best response to my beautiful homemade Coronation Chicken I had slaved in the kitchen to lovingly produce. I was determined to get them to at least try it.

In a moment of inspiration, I decided to tell them the story of how this traditional British delicacy was invented for Queen Elizabeth II's coronation in 1953. We blasted out the coronation hymn, *Zadock the Priest,* and looked up pictures on the internet of the Queen being crowned. Before I knew it, the children were excitedly gobbling down their dinner. For the rest of that week they told everyone how they saw the Queen and ate her chicken!

There was no change to the food on offer but the reaction to it was completely different. Through better communication I had got my children to put their misconceptions to one side and really understand the message, which in this instance was "Eat your dinner".

When you strip back everything else the one main function of a network marketer is to communicate. We need to share our message with prospects, customers and our teams. If you don't do this, you don't have a business. The more effective your communication becomes, the more successful you will be.

The fight for people's attention

Businesses are speaking, but how people are listening is changing. The strategy to capture people's attention is going to have to change. For the

2017 television broadcast of the United States Super Bowl, the price tag of a half time commercial was US$5.6 million. According to digital agency Essence, they achieved the same reach and impact through seventeen Snapchat sponsored campaigns run at the same time. The cost of Snapchat was estimated at around US$329,400.[52] Traditional forms of advertising are changing.

Many organisations are now moving their advertisements online, but this is also becoming less effective. Business Insider reported in the same year that 'ad blocking' online was up 30 percent on the previous year. This meant that consumers had programmed 615 million devices to block all forms of advertising popping up.[53] Even if the ads are getting through, fewer people appear to be responding.

One method of communication is breaking through more than ever. James Naughton, Chief of Staff at Zappos confirmed that,

> "Study after study show word of mouth, or personal recommendation to be the most effective form of convincing someone to buy a product."[54]

As a network marketer you are in the right place at the right time.

Leading brand and media strategists confirm this saying, "People are the new media… 92 percent of people trust recommendations from friends and family more than all other forms of marketing".[54]

Network marketing is perfect word of mouth communication. With the right message not only can we cut through the noise of the media, but we also already have a relationship with our prospects. They are more than likely to be people who know, like and trust us. We are perfectly placed to grow a business.

Communicating your company message

This may sound like a silly question, but what is it that your company actually does? What is it that you do and why is that important to you?

"Many growth minded people didn't plan to go to the top. They got there as a result of doing what they love. It's ironic: the top is where the fixed mindset people hunger to be, but it is where many growth minded arrive as a by-product of their enthusiasm for what they do.[49]*"*

—Dr Carol Dweck

Dale Partridge is the co-founder of 'Sevenly', one of Forbes magazine's fastest growing social good start-ups. He was convinced that the mission of his company was to 'Do Good'. They had been using this as a strap line for many years, however, when they went through a rebranding exercise this ethos was challenged. They realised that 'doing good' was not what they actually stood for. When Partridge and his team started to dig a little deeper they discovered doing good was just part of their story. Their real company cause was that 'People Matter'.

"Our team went back to the drawing board, this time asking more profound questions than before... Our business was like a complex system of roads, but every path originated from the same source: a conviction about the value of the individuals who made our company possible."[55]

Often in network marketing we communicate the value that our company teaches us. This is more than likely to be a perfectly good value but for you to be really passionate and talk about your company cause with authenticity it has to align with your beliefs and values.

Perhaps you offer a service to your customers and your network focuses on how that service saves people money. It would be easy to talk about saving money, but what if you dug a little deeper. You might find that what aligns with your values is that you're making people's lives easier so they don't have to worry about always hunting for the best deal.

Maybe you promote a product that helps your customers lose weight. The real company cause that might align with your values and beliefs is how that product gives your customers confidence to be themselves. It could be that the product enables them to feel comfortable enough in their own skin so they can find the perfect partner.

It is important to clarify that this does not mean the cause your company has been teaching you is wrong. It is simply not *your* cause.

Once I understood my values and had a comprehensive list of benefits - as discussed in Chapter 7 - I started to consider my company cause much more deeply. I began to see a different picture, exactly like Partridge. I kept asking why. Why do we do what we do? Why does that benefit our customers? Why is that important? This was an uncomfortable and sometimes quite frustrating process, but as I have mentioned before; no one ever has a breakthrough in their comfort zone! After much grey matter went into the subject I finally grasped my company cause with complete commitment.

I knew I had found my company cause because I talked with real passion and excitement about it. But also, another really exciting thing happened; all of a sudden my fear of talking to people about our customer proposition disappeared. In the introduction of this book, I mentioned how most people are too scared to talk to people about their business. They want to build a business, but appear to be too frightened to tell anyone, which is a pretty big barrier in network marketing. I believe this is because they have not found and connected with their company cause. Once they find the angle that aligns with their own values, these barriers begin to disintegrate.

How do you find your company cause? You are going to need to learn a skill called first principle thinking. It was originally cited by the ancient Greek philosopher Aristotle thousands of years ago, but proves as powerful today as it was then.[56] And many great leaders use this principle of thinking today.

Business legend Elon Musk credited many of his scientific and business breakthroughs to first principle thinking.

"You boil things down to the most fundamental truths ...and then reason up from there."[57]

Rather than simply accepting things for how they are, you keep going back and asking why things are how they are. Eventually, this takes you back until you can go no further and you have found your first principles. This is the process Dale Partridge went through and the process I followed. It is incredibly powerful and often reveals really interesting results. First principle thinking is an incredibly valuable skill to learn and something that will serve you many times if you commit to it.

You can use the same exercise for the industry cause. Why is the network marketing opportunity important to you? Using first principle thinking, I discovered that what the network marketing really meant to me was I could fix one of my frustrations. I was meeting all these amazing women who had phenomenal skills. However, by having children they were being made redundant. Their successful careers did not fit around their children. They had skills and abilities that would benefit the world, but there were very limited options for them to use them. The cause of the industry for me became about empowering these amazing ladies to fulfil their potential while still having the family choices they wanted.

Simon Sinek is known for decoding the most effective communication method. He called it the Golden Circle. “Every organisation - and every person’s career - operates on three levels... What we do, how we do it and why we do it”.[58] “Leading with WHY has a deeper, more emotional and ultimately more influential value”.[58]

The most effective way to communicate is with ‘why’. The ultimate why is when you find your highest value cause. When you learn to communicate this succinctly and effectively, you will find you begin to connect with people so they want to listen and engage with you.

Review your values and list of benefits. Identify the benefits you are most passionate about and start asking, “Why?” Why is that important? Why does that benefit the customer? Once you have answered this, ask yourself why again! Why is the answer to your first question true? Keep asking why until you can go no further back!

This can be a challenging exercise, but stick with it and go back to it another time if you struggle on the first attempt. If you are on your own doing this, a good tool can be to use your mobile telephone to voice record yourself talking about it. When you have to talk it through out loud it is amazing how much more can come out, than when you ponder quietly. Afterwards, you can also listen to the recording of yourself. Again, you will be amazed at the things you said, which you didn’t realise at the time. This can help your thought process continue further.

This can also be a great exercise to do with other people. Set the boundaries first and agree how much you are going to challenge each other. For the person doing the questioning - as tempting as it may be - never help answer any of the questions for your interviewee. The answers have to come from them because it is about what is important to them.

Speak to people

There is no getting away from it, to be successful in network marketing you have to speak to people. The only thing that stands between you and where you want to take your network marketing business is a number of conversations. The longer you put off these conversations, the further you delay your progress.

Talking about their business effectively is something many network marketers find difficult. As we identified previously, much of this concern comes from the knowledge that you are earning money from your loved ones. That is why communicating with your cause is much more powerful - and probably more interesting - for your audience. As network marketers, our main function is to act like disciples; to spread the word about the good we do and gain support. Exactly like the disciples in the Bible, one of the best ways we can do this is by telling stories about our causes.

Tell stories

TOMS shoes is an example of a company who 'are succeeding at this volatile moment in capitalism'. They have a story that fuels their business. The founder, Blake Mycoskie decided to form the company when travelling through Argentina. He saw many children suffering from blisters, foot sores and infections because they didn't have any shoes. He wanted to help them so he considered starting a charity to send shoes out to these children.

But Mycoskie then had a better idea. He decided to start a company that produced alpargata shoes, a soft canvas shoe worn throughout Argentina. Bingo, his business had a cause right at its heart. He marketed the shoes in developed countries with the promise that for every pair of shoes sold, his company delivered a pair of shoes to a child in need. TOMS was born and it was 'about a promise - a better tomorrow'.[59]

If you want to get people's attention and want them to listen, you need to talk about your network marketing business in terms of stories. The most powerful stories will be about your cause; whether that is a personal

> *"The giving component of TOMS makes our shoes more than a product. They're part of a story, a mission, a movement anyone can join... People who tell the TOMS story are more than just our customers, they're our supporters... Supporters beat customers every time.*[59]*"*
>
> —Blake Mycoskie

or team cause, or perhaps the cause of the industry. Exactly like Mycoskie you are looking for supporters. Think about the stories you can tell. Even if your cause is about the industry how can you tell that story?

Communicate with a buzz

Picture this; two pop up shelters, two displays, next to each other. One was buzzing with a crowd huddled around, the other had two miserable looking people slumped behind a plastic table. I didn't initially notice the second display as I walked up the High Street. I was too focused on trying to find out what was attracting so many people to the other stand. Why was everyone excitedly talking and gathering around?

The abandoned shelter had been set up and staffed to gain signatures for a local petition. The crowded shelter was selling tickets for a local amateur dramatic society's latest production. While their causes were different, there was more to the disproportionate levels of interest for the stands. I had seen other theatre groups selling tickets on the High Street and usually they too looked abandoned. What had made the difference on this day were the people running the stand and how they were communicating. I stood back and watched for a while.

The couple selling the tickets were visibly excited. They were almost bouncing around. When the crowds dispersed I saw clearly that they were having a great time and were passionate about what they were doing. They had energy, they had a buzz and it appeared magnetising. Their cheery chatter drew people in. People wanted to find out what was making this couple so excited on a damp cold morning. As one person diverted to go and investigate, then other people followed.

The energy and passion you use when communicating about your business will have a huge impact on how effective it is. When you find a cause you truly believe in you will find it is much easier to develop that magnetising buzz. People will feel the passion and they will be drawn to you. Everyone wants to be part of a tribe doing something important. Whether you are communicating about your products, opportunity or cause, make sure you do it like the amateur dramatics ticketers, not like the signature collectors.

"Great leaders create movements by empowering the tribe to communicate. They establish the foundation of people to make connections, as opposed to follow them.[60]"

—Seth Godin

Social media

If used correctly social media can be a great tool to help build your network marketing business. If used incorrectly you risk alienating your friends. In social and traditional media there is a fight for people's attention. You don't want to be seen participating in that battle. People switch off when they feel they are being sold to.

"Why wouldn't you join us?" she kept asking in the excruciating six minute video.

"I love the products, they are great. You will love them too".

"They cost only £79 for the starter kit".

"Why wouldn't you want to buy that?"

She looked uncomfortable and nervous, I could barely watch. Six months prior, this lovely lady appeared to be a normal Mum! Then, she joined a network marketing business. She had obviously been encouraged to hijack her Facebook account to promote an endless stream of adverts for her company. Every day there was a new picture of a product, a video of her talking about them, or a special offer graphic. The poor girl had obviously been encouraged to do this by her upline and while I am sure she got the odd sale, at what cost?

I scrolled back to a year prior and looked at some stats. Before she started her business, she posted the odd picture of the kids, being out with her friends and occasionally she shared an amusing video. Now it had all changed. If you had the patience to scroll through all her business adverts you can find a few pictures of the kids, but there had been a big shift. A year ago she was getting around fifty to one hundred 'likes' for each of her posts. Now, even for pictures of her cute kids they were down to about five to ten 'likes'. Plus, when I dug a little deeper, it appeared that those five to ten 'likes' were all from people involved in the same business as her.

While it is wonderful to see people passionate to build a network marketing business, in my opinion this is completely the wrong strategy. Not only does it damage the reputation of the person making the post, but it also damages the industry. If our businesses were easy to build by advertising on social media, our companies would do away with their networks and advertise directly themselves. Yes, they wouldn't have us as their brand and they would probably hire some lush celebrity to attract people instead!

The best way to approach social media is to remember that it is meant to be social, not sales. Never on my personal Facebook page do I sell my business directly. The most powerful way to use social media is to promote your cause. Show the good that you are doing for the world and the people watching will be attracted to connect with you.

Everyone wants to be part of something greater than themselves and make an impact on the world. When they see you working towards a cause - even if it is in a small way - their trust for you builds. This is about relationships and communication.

On my personal Facebook page I continue to prominently post pictures of my children and the fun stuff we get up to. Stippled between this will be several business lifestyle posts; pictures of me with the amazing business team having a blast together, updates from our cause and occasionally little congratulatory stories for team members who inspire me. I am not promoting, I am telling the story of my life in the hope that other people will want to connect with me and be part of that with me.

Of course, this is not only a one way relationship. I also comment, like and connect through private messages with my other Facebook friends. I want to share and actively participate in their lives so we build relationships and are not simply spectators.

If you succeed in social media, not merely Facebook but on other platforms as well, occasionally acquaintances will contact you directly, but more often than not you will need to make the first step. No matter how clever you are with social media, network marketing will always be about picking up the telephone and actually talking to people. It will always be about real human connections and in a noisy world, that is our strength.

Team communication

I noticed how our company provided fantastic online training, but I also noticed that many of the team were not engaging with it. However, when

I ran a live online video training they tuned in, engaged and learnt. Why was this? The company training is significantly better produced, while mine can bounce around as ideas ping out of my head. Company training is on demand while people have to awkwardly tune in to mine while they are driving home from work or feeding the kids.

The difference was all to do with connection. Communicating with your network is not enough, that communication has to have connection at its core. My team prefer to learn from me because they know, like and trust me. They feel emotionally connected because we have built relationships with each other. Communication is a two way process.

The only way to communicate and build relationships is to talk to your team. Texting, WhatsApp and emails won't cut it. People need to hear the expression in your voice and you need to hear it in theirs. You can learn more from someone's expression than you can from the words they use. When talking, a conversation can flow organically and will often go off on tangents. Exploring these tangents is where you will find out what is really important to the people you are working with.

I measure the success of my activity on the number of minutes I use on my mobile telephone. In a typical month, I will make thousands of outgoing calls and receive as many inbound. I have tracked these numbers for several years and unsurprisingly they correlate directly to the growth of my business. It is worth investing in a good wireless hands-free kit. I can often be found emptying the dishwasher or folding the washing while chatting away.

When you talk to your team it is not only about finding out how they are progressing their business, it is finding out about them. It is about building friendships and deep meaningful relationships. What is going on in their lives? How are they feeling about their families? What worries them? What are they excited about? You want to have a team of friends, not a team of business partners.

Face to face conversation is more powerful than talking on the telephone.

Spending time with your team building relationships will not only help your business, it is one of the most fulfilling parts of what we do.

There will always be a place to harness the communication technologies. Within my business I use many WhatsApp groups and frequent video messages. This type of group messaging helps the team pull together and build consistent camaraderie. Where people go wrong is when they use these as a replacement for actually talking.

Create the culture of communication within your team and enjoy all the wonderful relationships you will build.

"The belief is that 55% of communication is body language, 38% is the tone of voice and 7% is the actual words spoken.[61]*"*

—Psychology Today, 2011

Part Four

RESULTS

[Our business is about relationships—REAL human connections—not more noise in an overcrowded market.]

[Chapter 11] CONNECTION

As an adult I present myself as a motivated and confident woman. People see me as a leader, a natural networker and someone who has it all worked out; the expert of connection. But what is the real truth?

As a child I was insular, quiet and reserved. Qualities I see every day painfully reflected in my young son. I know he will be okay, but watching him negotiate life reminds me of the challenges I had with friendships and above all, connection. Connection didn't come naturally to me. I was the geeky loner at school, but with the geek part replaced with dyslexia! I was the odd one out in my family and I never felt I fitted in anywhere.

As I grew up I found a coping mechanism for this awkwardness. I discovered that by getting busy and being successful I earned respect from people. I used this to gain connection through a back door, whether it was representing sport nationally, rising through the ranks of volunteer organisations, or gaining work promotions. From the outside it appeared that I was always succeeding. Because of my success it seemed I was fully connected. Whatever I set my mind to, I found a cause and the motivation to rise to the top of my game. But every time I got to the top, I lacked the one yearning I was searching for, a deep meaningful connection; that was until I found network marketing.

What we have in network marketing is so powerful, but we are frustrated because we are not truly harnessing it. The laws of physics define that everything is always moving. If you are not moving forward, then by default you are moving backwards. Now is the time to take the next big step forward in our industry. Now is the time to harness our unique power... connection.

Network marketing connection

Through reading this book you have learned:

- The new challenges of the world that we live in today
- How network marketing is poised to perfectly serve that world
- How network marketing meets the desires of flexible money, belonging, and fulfilment
- How engaging a cause supported by your culture, commitment and communication can be the tools for success.

The measure of whether this is pulling together and achieving is connection.

> Connection is both the measure of your success *and* your reward.

When you feel a deep and meaningful connection to your business, the industry, your team, your prospects and your cause, you will be moving forward towards your goals.

The stronger that connection, the faster you will move. It is the most powerful asset our businesses have. By ensuring your business generates connection you can have the success you are looking for.

The opportunity

In the rest of the world, most:

- Companies have cheap connection,

in the form of ignored advertisements

» Employees have cheap connection, only valued for the job they perform and have to be paid for.

» Friendships have cheap connection from superficial Facebook likes.

As network marketers we need to be cautious we don't follow the rest of the market and fall into these traps of cheap connection. We could be building our businesses through shallow social media messages or driving our team towards targets, but if we did this we would be missing the real power of what we have.

Unlocking the connection in network marketing is how you unlock the real success.

Network marketing can be different:

» The unique sales proposition of our business model is that we have something much more powerful than shouting sales messages. We have real human beings with real relationships. We have a way to meaningfully cut through the noise and connect with our prospects.

» Network marketing has a business opportunity that gives much more than merely wages. It develops people to be the best they can be. It gives them something to belong to that is greater than themselves. Business partners can feel belonging, fulfilment and above all else, connection to something really worthwhile.

» By sharing the amazing journey of building a network marketing business we build relationships of deep connection with our compatriots.

» By being part of network marketing, we

> are standing up together for something more important than ourselves. This brings us closer together and connects us to those people willing to come on this amazing journey. The relationships you will personally build through network marketing will become one of the most valuable assets you own.

To harness the power of what we have, we have to harness the connection.

Currency

Connection is a currency because there is no limit to the amount of connection you can earn. You can start with very little and work your way up to earning more and more. By following the process of implementing the 4Cs, you will begin to create your own Connection Currency.

When you want to become richer in connection you need to stretch yourself, raise your cause and start the cycle again. The more Connection Currency you earn the more money, belonging and fulfilment you will earn.

The key to your success lies in your connection.

The real value of our businesses

It is fair to say it took several years for my family to take me and my 'part time little business' seriously. It was only after my business was turning over customer sales in the millions of pounds did the value of what I have start to become apparent.

One day, I was talking with my father and for a change he was asking me the questions! He had always warned me that as a woman I would probably have to choose between raising children and a career. I suspect the fact I had gained the best of both worlds shocked him and maybe made him a little proud!

As he questioned the ins and outs of network marketing he concluded it really was a fabulous business model except for one thing. Ownership.

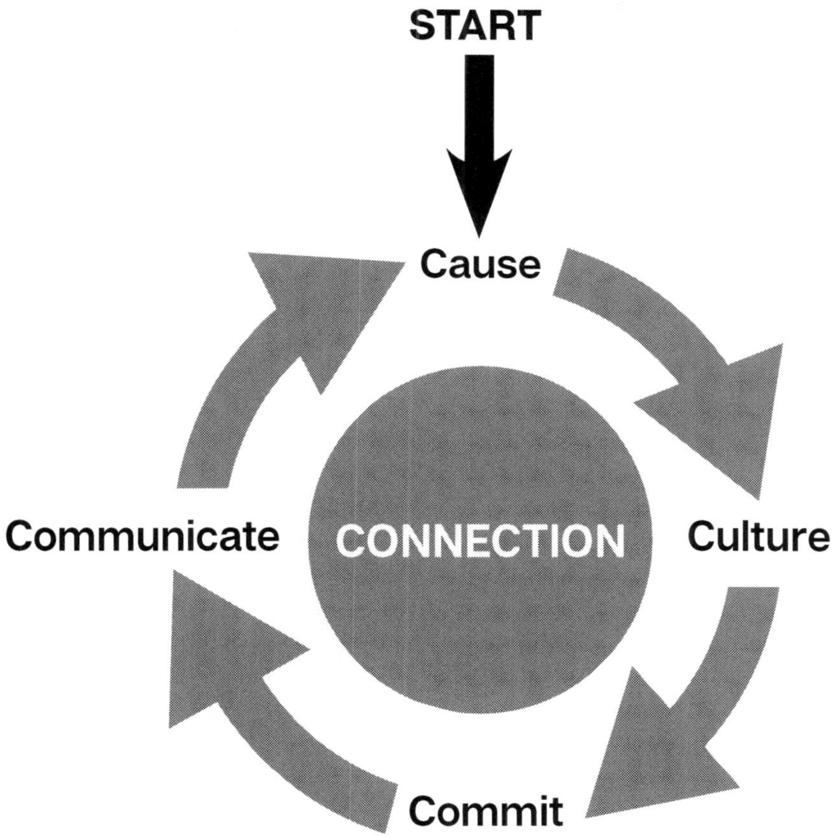
START
Cause
Culture
Commit
Communicate
CONNECTION

He warned that while I had security of my own distributorship, if the company decided to sell or close I had no real power. I could lose everything.

He was right, but he missed one important fact. I had an asset so much more valuable than the amazing opportunity my company offered. I had connection.

As we discussed earlier in the book, network marketing is not about the products or the services we offer... it is about the people. I had connected with my business and changed as a person. I had built a team of people who had become a family. I had meaningful relations with so many amazing distributors. These were things that no one could take away from me.

If I had only built my business as a sales enterprise and never invested in real connection, it would not be nearly as valuable as it is today. I have complete security in my business because I am surrounded by the most awesome people, and whatever happens, we will always stick together. Not only does this bring us a greater sense of belonging and fulfilment, it is also quite profitable!

If you want real, long-term success and security in your business you need to start measuring your business in terms of connections as well. You will know when you are on the road to achieving success in network marketing because you will feel connected.

However, I promised at the start of this book that there were no magic pills or quick fixes. Implementing the 4Cs won't change your business over night. Connection is not only something you decide about, it is something you must prove to yourself and other people. True, deep, meaningful, rich connection takes time and effort to create. That is why it becomes such a valuable asset.

Connection as a measurement

You need to become more aware of your Connection Currency and start measuring how connected you are. It is quite emotive because connection is based on feelings, but there are certain questions you can ask yourself to make sure you are on the right tracks.

■ Cause measured in connection

» Do you have a cause that you are passionate about?

» Do you feel connected to the cause of your company and the industry?

» How connected do you feel to these causes?

» Is that connection strong enough that you are motivated?

The deeper the emotional connection you have to your cause, the more engaged you will feel. If you have not yet found a cause that raises this emotion, this is a great place to start earning your Connection Currency.

■ Culture measured in connection

» How connected do you feel to your personal and team culture?

» Is this a culture you have consciously moulded?

» Do your team members engage and connect to your culture?

» Does your culture align and connect to your values?

If you are developing a culture within your team, which gives them a sense of security and belonging, you will have good Connection Currency. Your culture will become a tool to attract prospects to your business rather than repel them.

■ Commitment measured in connection

» Are you connected enough to your business that you are willing to step out of your comfort zone?

» Are you committed to building the connections and relationships with other people in the business?

» Are you willing to make conscious sacrifices to connect with your business?

Network marketing is hard work and requires real commitment. When you feel connected to your business, that hard work begins to feel fun and incredibly rewarding. Eventually, it stops feeling like work and becomes the most fulfilling lifestyle. There will be challenges. It will not be a fairy tale. Embrace the fact that for every hurdle you overcome, the deeper your connection with your business will be.

■ Communication measured in connection

» If you are communicating with prospects through sales messages on social media, your connection is going to be cheap and your long-term rewards will reflect that. However, if you are using communication as a tool to build relationships with integrity, you will be earning more currency.

» How do you communicate with your prospects?

» If you are communicating with your team about targets and hollow promotions, your Connection Currency is cheap. If you are gaining a deep understanding and empathy for your team members' lives, your currency is rich?

» How do you communicate with your team?

Of course, there will always be a time to talk about targets and actually ask for the business to make a sale, but only once a connection has been made. Once you have a connection, asking the direct questions becomes easier and natural. If you feel unable to ask these questions, go back to developing the connection first.

Skills matter

It's still very important to learn the skills of our industry. Please don't misunderstand that what we have learned up until this point in our network marketing evolution will always be incredibly important. To be successful you need to continue to learn the 'how to' of building a network marketing business. There are the most phenomenal resources available in our industry to help you learn all the skills you need.

Make sure you perform these skills with connection at the centre.

Be the change

In January 2013, sixteen of the world's most influential business leaders gathered together around a boardroom table, including Richard Branson, Arianna Huffington, Paul Polman and Professor Muhammed Yunus, to name a few. They decided they wanted to change the world, but they knew they couldn't do it on their own. They needed a little help from their friends.

This meeting was the founding event of 'The B Team', a not-for-profit organisation that has been set up to help change the way the world does business. "Founded in the belief that the private sector can, and must, redefine both its responsibilities and its own terms of success, we are developing a Plan B – for concerted, positive action that will ensure business becomes a driving force for social, environmental and economic benefit".[62]

In the few short years since The B Team was launched it has achieved a huge amount of success. They identified ten key goals where they wanted to make an impact and are now having significant, measured success in each of these areas. Hundreds of other businesses, small and large, are joining The B Team. More than three thousand companies have registered with the organisation as Benefit Corporations agreeing to be accountable to their stakeholders, as well as shareholders and aligning to the principles of The B Team. [63]

While this is only the beginning, none of this would have been possible without the coming together of a group of people who wanted to see a change.

I have a vision and I want to see a change in our industry, but I need your help! As we stand at the dawn of a new era for our amazing industry, I have a cause and I want every single one of you to be part of it.

Through this book we have learned how perfectly placed our industry is to do so much good in the lives of many different people. At the moment we are not fulfilling our potential, but never has there been a better time to harness the real power of what we have. The power of connection.

I want you to join me in an evolution of our industry from network marketing to Connection Marketing.

Together, we can transform our industry to utilise its real power; an industry that is going to change the world through connection. The more of us who unite in this new way of thinking and acting, the bigger the impact we can make will be. I want us all to be overwhelmingly rich in Connection Currency, pulling together in the cause of Connection Marketing.

Take Action

The next step is to take action.

Firstly, take personal action. Discover your cause, develop your culture, commit to your business and communicate what you are doing and why you are doing it. I implore you to start applying the principles of the Connection Currency right now. Start your Connection Marketing journey and begin your success.

However, if this is truly going to be a journey of connection you should not be on your own. Join together with other people in your team, other people in your network, and other people in different networks. Join together in a new community of Connection Marketing.

This is not going to happen overnight, but if we evolve together, if we connect, we can change our industry and change the world. If you are ready to make the change and if you are ready to make a meaningful difference, now is the time.

The world is waiting for us to show them the way.

Welcome to a new world of Connection Marketing.

JOIN THE CONNECTION MARKETING COMMUNITY…

go to

www.connectionmarketing.global

CONNECT WITH THE AUTHOR

Email: fran@fran.global

Website: www.fran.global

Facebook: @FranBGlobal

Twitter: @FranBGlobal

Instagram: @FranBGlobal

LinkedIn: @FranBGlobal

REFERENCES AND FURTHER READING

Chapter 3

1 Maslow, A (1943), *A Theory of Human Motivation, Psychological Review*

2 Alter, A (2017), *Irresistible; The Rise of Addictive Technology* and the *Business of Keeping Us Hooked,* London: Vintage

3 W J Schroeder, *Social Marketing*; online https://goo.gl/c3SqjV

4 Direct Selling Association (2017), *Direct Selling in 2016: An Overview*; online https://goo.gl/dd25KE

5 Urban, T (2017), *Why Generation Y Yuppies Are Unhappy*; Huffington Post; online https://goo.gl/ZsMnLt

6 Carnegie, D (1953), *How to Win Friends and Influence People*, Reading: Vermillion

7 Deloitte, (2017), *The Deloitte Millennial Survey 2017*, online https://goo.gl/6eg1oi

8 Stillman, D; Stillman J (2017), *Gen Z @ Work*, New York: Harper Business

9 Millennial Branding (2014), Internships.com Study, online https://goo.gl/TLJG6u

10 The Centre For Generational Kinetics, (2017), *The State of Gen Z 2017*, online https://goo.gl/RYCQ9K

11 Desjardins J (2017), *Here's what the world's $63 trillion in government debt looks like, Business Insider UK,* online https://goo.gl/VFZ5xJ

12 Porter, M (2013), *The Case for Letting Business Solve Social Problems*; video online https://goo.gl/M5HYQq

13 Matyszczyk, C (2014), *Obama: Social media makes us see how messy the world is,* CNet, online https://goo.gl/YAzSUd

14 Elkington, J (1997), *Cannibals with Forks*, Oxford: Capstone

15 Mycoskie, B (2011), *Start Something That Matters*, New York: Ebury

16 Mitra, S (2013), *Build a School in the Clouds*; video online https://goo.gl/G7gr13

17 Ryan, L (2017), *Job Security is Disappearing*, Forbes Magazine; online https://goo.gl/ekZqCZ

18 Weinlick, J (2017), *What Does it Mean that Job Security is Disappearing*, online https://goo.gl/8QkfMa

19 McKinsey Global Institute (2017), *Jobs Lost, Jobs Gained: Workforce Transitions in a time of Automation;* online https://goo.gl/RCihcq

20 The Balance (2017), *How Outsourcing Jobs Affects the U.S. Economy*; online https://goo.gl/5UrCqI

21 Inman, P (2016), *More than 900,000 UK workers now on zero-hours contracts*, The Guardian; online https://goo.gl/u9zkyE

22 McCarthy, N (2017), *Which Countries Have The Most and Least Con-*

fidence in Their Governments? Forbes Magazine; online https://goo.gl/HhH9U7

Chapter 4

23 Spriggs, R (1975), *The Fables of Aesop*, London: Book Club Associates

Chapter 5

24 Selinger, J; O'Connor, S; Wong, J; Donelan J (2015), *Humans Can Continuously Optimize Energetic Cost During Walking, Current Biologies*; online https://goo.gl/gWvCc3

25 Fiske, S; Taylor, S (1991), *Social Cognition*, New York: McGraw-Hill

26 Oaklander, M (2015), *Here's Proof That You Are Wired to Be Lazy,* Time Magazine; online https://goo.gl/I9brgL

27 Pink, D (2009), *Drive*, Edinburgh: Canongate

28 Ariely, D (2016), *Payoff*, London: Simon & Schuster

29 Wikipedia (2017), Band Aid (band); online https://goo.gl/nAsRvi

30 The Sunday Times (2017), *Rich List*; online https://goo.gl/Usku6H

31 The Oxford Dictionary (2017), *Definition Cause* online https://goo.gl/AsnfJE

32 The Oxford Dictionary (2017), *Definition Charity*; online https://goo.gl/NZDhZj

33 Armstrong, J (2015), *Football Fan leaves non-league club more than £300,000 in will*, The Mirror; online https://goo.gl/6sO6O9

Chapter 6

34 Willard, B (2002), *The Sustainability Advantage*, Gabriola Island: New Society

35 Roser, M (2017), *War and Peace, Our World in Data*; online https://goo.gl/VFT8xo

36 Roser, M; Ritchie, H (2017), *Natural Catastrophes, Our World in Data*; online https://goo.gl/9FoM1F

37 Aziz, A; Jones, B (2016), *Good is the New Cool*, New York; Regan Arts

38 Schwartz, D (2016), *The Magic of Thinking Big*, London: Vermillion

Chapter 7

39 Sinek, S (2011), *Start with Why*, London: Penguin

40 Covey, S (1989), *The 7 Habits of Highly Effective People*, London: Simon & Schuster

41 The Oxford Dictionary (2017), *Definition Value*; online https://goo.gl/1YFUmf

42 Demartini, J (2013), *The Values Factor*, London: Penguin

43 Charity:Water (2017), *Our Progress*; online https://goo.gl/N6pUAM

Chapter 8

44 Lacy, S (2009), *Amazon Buys Zappos*, Techcrunch; online https://goo.gl/hvWUFP

45 Hsieh, T (2011), *Delivering Happiness*, New York: Grand Central

46 Sinek, S (2014), *Leaders Eat Last*, London: Penguin

Chapter 9

47 Dolan, P (2014), *Happiness by Design*, London: Penguin

48 Duckworth, A (2017), *Grit*, London: Penguin

49 Dwek, C (2006), *Mindset*, London: Little Brown

50 Gladwell, M (2008), *Outliers*, London: Penguin

51 Hunt-Davies, B; Beveridge, H (2012), *Will it Make the Boat Go Faster*, Leicester: Troubador

Chapter 10

52 Heine, C (2017), *12 Really Intriguing Digital Marketing Stats From This Week,* Adweek; online https://goo.gl/ntqk1F

53 O'Reilly, L (2017), *Ad blocker usage is up 30%,* Business Insider UK; online https://goo.gl/9bxZF2

54 Aziz, A; Jones, B (2016), *Good is the New Cool*, New York; Regan Arts

55 Partridge, D (2015), *People Over Profit*, Nashville: Nelson

56 Irwin, T (1990), *Aristotle's First Principles,* New York: Oxford University Press

57 Rose, K (2013), *The First Principles Method Explained by Elon Musk*; video online https://goo.gl/o2XNwJ

58 Sinek, S; Mead, D; Docker, P (2017), *Find Your Why*, London: Penguin

59 Mycoskie, B (2011), *Start Something That Matters*, New York: Ebury

60 Godin, S (2008), *Tribes*, London: Little Brown

61 Thompson, J (2011), *Is Nonverbal Communication a Numbers Game?* Psychology Today; online https://goo.gl/BUOZPt

Chapter 11

62 The B Team (2017), *About*, online https://goo.gl/r5qKkm

63 The B Team (2016), *Towards a Plan B for Business*, online https://goo.gl/nrmyFj

DEDICATION

To my two amazing children
O and A
who inspire me every day.

ACKNOWLEDGEMENTS

Mum and Dad, for your endless inspiration and grounding. For showing me the opportunities of life and teaching me the commitment to achieve them.

Chris Boorman, for many years of amazing support and growth together. For being an amazing Daddy to our two little people and for always being willing to step up and help out.

Lu, Nick and *Al,* for helping form who I am and always supporting me from a place of such love.

Joe Redston, for the support with my extrovert thinking. For listening, stretching me and helping me believe in myself.

Joga Shoker, for being the best buddy a girl could have, not only in the business but outside of it too.

Karen Young, without you none of this would have ever started. You gave me the best possible beginning to my business and I will always be thankful.

Steve Critchley and *Keith Bassi,* for your wonderful friendship and up-line support over the years.

Our *UW Family,* our amazing team, for all your commitment and dedication which is what keeps me loving the journey every day. You are so much more than a team. You are part of my family. Thank you to each and every one of you who has shared this journey together... so far!

Simon Goodwin, Joanna Williams and *Chetna Reay,* my Beta readers, for your feedback which was invaluable.

Barry Phillips, Wendy Yorke, Meg Martin, Lisa Knight and *Heather Horsley* in the production of the final book.

ABOUT THE AUTHOR

Fran Boorman has an impressive history of building a network marketing business to turnover in excess of £8 million, around her young family. With ten years' experience in the industry, she is consistently recognised as one of the top performers within her company.

Partnered with a top British PLC, Fran speaks regularly at many events and trainings in front of audiences of more than 4,000 people.

Prior to starting network marketing, Fran achieved a first class honours degree in Industrial Design and went on to build and sell a successful online craft business.

She is a shareholder and a second generation family business owner, giving her extensive experience of board level management. She has been invited to be a Non-Executive Director for a number of different companies.

One of her passions is setting up charities in developing countries. Aged 21, Fran ran her first international expedition to a rural part of Uganda. A key aim of this expedition was to develop the engagement and leadership of the participants. This proved incredibly successful and more than a decade later, the legacy of this first project continues.

Passionate about giving back, Fran continues to run these expeditions and utilises them as a vehicle to help individuals and organisations learn how they can increase employee engagement through developing a purpose-driven business.

In her spare time, Fran is a keen skier, having competed at an international level as a teenager. She also loves trail running, hiking, travelling and pretty much any activity that takes place outside.

28169608R00088

Printed in Great Britain
by Amazon